Three Plays
for Small Classes

by

Vivian Jones Schmidt

Printed with support from the Waldorf Curriculum Fund

Published by:
Waldorf Publications at the
Research Institute for Waldorf Education
38 Main Street
Chatham, NY 12037

Title: *Three Plays for Small Classes*
Author: Vivian Jones Schmidt
Proofreader: Ruth N. Riegel
Layout: Ann Erwin
Cover image: Vivian Jones Schmidt

© 2016 Waldorf Publications
ISBN 978-1-943582-03-7

Contents

Introduction.................................. 5

A Merry Adventure of Robin Hood................ 7

The Philosopher's Stone....................... 40

The Silver Slippers........................... 72

Introduction

Finding the courage to write a play requires both inspiration and a certain amount of desperation. As middle school classes, particularly in young schools, often consist of seven or eight students, the desperation comes with the territory. Hundreds of already published plays are available for this age group, but rarely does one find a pre-published play that appropriately meets the developmental and curricular needs of a small Waldorf class. This was the situation I faced in both my second and third classes. Every class was expected to present a play, every year, at both schools. I studied a lot of plays before coming to the conclusion that I would have to write my own.

The first play in this volume, "A Merry Adventure of Robin Hood," was written for a sixth grade class. As I looked around for an inspiration that would align with the Roman/Medieval history theme of the year, I picked up Llancelyn Green's *Robin Hood*. Immediately, images of my students in the various roles appeared in my mind, and I knew I had found the perfect source material.

The next year, seventh grade, the student mix was somewhat different but the size of the class was similar. Again, I sought inspiration in the curriculum. Seventh grade is the first year for chemistry in a Waldorf school, and the history theme is Renaissance/Reformation. Combining the two into a play about a search for "The Philosopher's Stone" seemed like a natural choice.

That class performed James Thurber's *Many Moons* as their eighth grade play, and I highly recommend it for a class of nine students [or eight students plus one adventurous math teacher], as its fairy-tale quality appeals to all ages. The next eighth grade I taught, however, had only seven students, so once again I was searching for an appropriate play. I shared my frustration with the class and asked for ideas. One student said, "What about *The Wizard of Oz*?" Knowing this class, if I had suggested this source, it would have been rejected out of hand. But as the idea came from a fellow student, they were immediately enthusiastic, so I agreed to study the story and see what I could do. The play, "The Silver Shoes," is the result.

Casting a play is always an interesting process. Some teachers simply assign parts, and some who assign parts do so out of their understanding of what it means to assign parts "pedagogically." Certainly a discussion of pedagogical assignments in class plays would be a welcome exploration. For example, is a role assigned because it reflects how that child is seen by peers or by teachers? Is it assigned to be the opposite of the child's apparent role in the class? My approach has always been as follows. We start reading through the play a few months before the performance date, devoting 20–30 minutes a day to the process. Each day, different students are assigned to read the various roles. After a few days, I ask the students if there are parts they have not read that they would like to, and each student gives me a list. When we've finished reading the play, I ask each student to give me a prioritized list of the four roles s/he is most interested in playing—plus a list assigning every student in the class to a role. Remarkably, these lists are very often so similar that, in the end, everyone [including the parents] is satisfied with the casting of the play. This approach avoids direct engagement with the question of "pedagogical casting," but interestingly, the assigned roles have always seemed to be both a reflection and an expansion of the students' basic classroom presence.

Is there anyone who doesn't love the process of working with and presenting a middle school play? Each rehearsal is a challenge, but the rehearsal process itself brings to light new and deeper levels of understanding of oneself and one's students as human beings on journeys of self-discovery. By the time the costumes and sets become priorities, the class has found a unity in its diversity—a unity that perhaps has never been present before. I hope that every teacher who finds something useful in these plays will also find something remarkable and inspirational in preparing for a performance. And, listen, if I can write a play, so can you.

– VIvian Jones Schmidt

A Merry Adventure of Robin Hood

Characters:
- Bishop
- Shariff
- Brother Aldric
- Sergeant
- Little John
- Will Scarlet
- Robin Hood
- Much
- Old Woman

[Players come onto stage from various locations within the hall. Standing on the stage and on the risers in seemingly random locations, they recite the Prologue.]

Prologue

Once, long ago, when the world seemed young,
Songs of adventure and mischief were sung
By minstrels who traveled from land to land
With tales in their hearts and harps in their hands.

They sang of brave knights on their chargers bold,
Of the ladies they loved, and their treasures of gold;
Of castles and palaces and tournaments,
Of costly garments, intoxicating scents;

Of kings and queens and the wars they fought,
Of those who did—and did not do—as they ought.
But of all these stories told 'round the hearth-fire,
The best told of a king and his faithful squire.

Folks called for the story of that rascal, Robin Hood,
And how he stayed loyal to King Richard the Good.
Again and again they asked for Robin's song—
How he tricked the Sheriff and the King's brother, John.

Now Richard languished in a prison far away
And John, his royal brother, seized the day
To rule dear England as his very own fief—
Some say as a tyrant, and some, as a thief.

For he pressed on the folk exorbitant tolls
Which forced them to lose their precious freeholds.
Even the wealthy were taxed beyond bearing
If they failed in obedience to Prince John and his daring.

One such lord was Robert, of Locksley Estate:
He refused Prince John, for on Richard he'd wait.
So John sent his Sheriff of Nottingham
To seize Lord Robert and all of his lands.

The young lord escaped to the forest of Sherwood—
And soon became known as Robin Hood.
There Robin, bold Robin, according to the lore,
Would rob the rich and give to the poor.

And now gentle ladies, good gentlemen, all,
We invite you to sit here in this great hall,
As we poor players, unworthy at best,
Enact a brief tale of Robin and his quest.

You'll learn how Robin, Little John, and Will Scarlet,
Encountered a rich man in poor churchly garments;
How they raised gold for Richard from that confused cleric
And how Robin confounded that scoundrel, the Sheriff.

For Robin aspired to aid Richard's release
From the prison he was kept in, far off to the East.
So he gathered a treasure of jewels and gold—
A true king's ransom, so the minstrels told.

But truer still was the devotion he guarded
As he fought for King Richard, the Lionhearted.

[Players exit, stage right (Bishop, Sheriff, Brother Aldric, Sergeant), and stage left (Little John, Robin Hood, Will Scarlet, Much, Old Woman).]

Act I, Scene 1

[Curtain opens partway to reveal a table. The Bishop, dressed in the rich robes of his office, sits behind the table, with Brother Aldric at his side. He is counting out piles of gold. The Sheriff watches, amused.]

Bishop: ... Seven and twenty, eight and twenty, nine and twenty... Brother Aldric, watch you my counting carefully. We would not want poor King Richard *[sarcastically]* to be at any loss on our account! Why, what if one of these coins were to be lost *[slips one into his pocket]*, or perhaps stolen *[slides one over to the Sheriff]* by some rogue? No, no, no! We must give a good accounting to our ruler!

Sheriff: I must say, Your Grace, that you do your figures quite well for a man of the cloth. *[slides another coin toward himself]* I had rather thought that you had sworn to a life of poverty when you took your vows in the Church.

Bishop: Ah! To be sure, as a youngster, I was wed to Lady Poverty. But as an important supporter of our noble Prince John, I must represent the benefits of that position to the lords hereabout—especially those who stubbornly refuse to swear fealty to John, holding that Richard will return. What nonsense! If our John has his way, Richard will languish in that German prison until his death, forgotten as befits a King who leaves his kingdom to fight on foreign soil. King John will never leave England.

Sergeant: Uh... excuse me, my lord, but it is Prince John, is it not? Or has some misfortunate accident befallen Richard, making John the King now?

Bishop: Of course you are correct, Sergeant. It was a mere slip of the tongue. For I cannot help but look forward to the days when we have a King in England once more, and I cannot help but favor John. His ways are much to my liking. Look you, he gave me the task of collecting taxes in our shire.

Sheriff [*sliding another coin into his pile*]: And did he also give you the task of lining your own pockets?

[Sergeant watches, befuddled.]

Bishop: Ahh—a most perspicacious question, my lord Sheriff. Our noble Prince John instructed me to collect a certain sum *in toto*, as we say in Latin. And, if I happened to collect more than that, why, it was clear that those sums would fund my work: my long hours here at this table, my forbearance in dealing with pleading peasants and lamenting lordlings, and my tremendous mathematical talents. *[The Bishop slaps the Sheriff's hand as he inches toward the gold once again.]*

Brother Aldric: Pardon me, my lord Sheriff, but one cannot expect my lord Bishop to calculate accurately if one continues to subtract from the sum he has so recently added. Perhaps if you would show favor to this pile...?

Bishop: Most insightful, most perspicacious, most wise, Brother Aldric!

Sheriff: And I shall most gladly, most humbly, comply!

Sergeant: Er... if I might be so bold, Your Honorship, what are you going to do with all this gold?

Sheriff [*kicking the Sergeant under the table*]: I'm sure what the Sergeant means, my lord, is to inquire as to whether or not you will need our assistance in protecting the gold you collect.

Bishop: But of course, dear Sheriff. After all, you have the right to be privy to whatever takes place within this Shire. As soon as I have completed my calculations, we shall pack up the proper amount and transport it to Nottingham, where the Prince's treasurer awaits us.

Sheriff: And how exactly do you plan to transport the gold, my lord?

Sergeant: Yes, how will you make sport of the gold?

Bishop [*looking at the Sergeant in a confused way*]: I have left such details to my assistant, Brother Aldric.

Brother Aldric: My lord Sheriff, if it please you, we plan to ride to Nottingham with a company of twenty men-at-arms, departing the Bishop's palace here at dawn on the morrow. If we ride at a good pace, we should be in Nottingham by nightfall.

Sheriff: Twenty men-at-arms, you say? Departing at dawn?

Brother Aldric: Correct, my lord Sheriff.

Sheriff: And may I inquire as to what influenced these plans?

Brother Aldric: But of course, my lord. Everyone knows that the outlaw they call Robin Hood haunts the forest of Sherwood. I am quite certain that I do not believe all one hears about this creature, but we must go well-protected for my lord Bishop's sake. Further, by leaving at dawn, we shall pass through Sherwood in the full light of day. With an armed and alert company about us, we shall have the advantage over any thief, and certainly over this so-called "king of Sherwood."

Sheriff: Hmmm. Well, in truth, your plan does have merit. *[pause, thoughtful.]* However, let me assure you that this Robin Hood does exist, and that he is most clearly ruler of all the outlaws who work their foul deeds within Sherwood Forest. Yes, you are quite correct in planning for protections. However *[raising his voice and banging his fist on the table]*, you could scarce have provided the scoundrel with greater notice of your errand had you hired trumpeters to herald the news of your presence!

Bishop: I beg your pardon, my lord Sheriff? What exactly is your meaning here? I trust my clerk implicitly.

Sheriff: Forgive me, my lord Bishop, for speaking so strongly. I am certain that Brother Aldric is most competent in matters related to the Church. However, do me the honor of trusting my competence in matters related to Sherwood and its resident outlaws. I assure you, this plan will accomplish nothing beyond alerting every reprobate within the Forest, and especially Robin Hood, to your presence—and to the fact that you must be on a mission of great importance, to warrant such a large company of armed men.

Bishop: Very well, my lord Sheriff, I grant you competence in your own affairs. But what would you have us do? Take to the forest paths with our feet, as if we were common beggars?

Sheriff: But that is exactly what I would have you do, my lord! It is a most brilliant plan! I congratulate you!

Sergeant: Yes! Conbobulations!

Bishop [*obviously flattered, but confused*]: I thank you for the compliment, my lord, but I remain in ignorance. How are we, unaccompanied and unprotected, to transport the gold?

Sheriff: My lord, often the simplest plan is truly the best. Only consider: What thief in his right mind would trouble himself with two mendicant friars, making their way from forest hut to forest hut, with their wooden bowls in their hands? Only conceal the gold about your persons. Dress yourself and your clerk in the plain brown robes of the begging friars. Take up the begging bowl. Slip out of your palace by the kitchen door—why, I do believe that even your own staff would not recognize you!

Bishop: Hmmm. Well, I confess that though I would be more at ease with an escort of armed men, your plan does seem to have some merit. I shall consider it.

Sheriff: Bear in mind, your Grace, that Robin Hood has far more than twenty men who await only his call to spring into action. And they are by far the best bowmen in the realm.

Brother Aldric: To be sure, your Grace, perhaps we should follow the Sheriff's advice. Perhaps he could lend security to the plan by following, with a few men, at a distance. Then, if we do fall into the outlaws' clutches, the Sheriff will be close at hand to lend us his aid.

Bishop: I concede. It shall be as you say, my lord Sheriff, with the addition of Brother Aldric's most intelligent suggestion. Do you see, Sheriff, why he is my clerk, why I trust him, in fact, above all others?

[*The curtain closes.*]

Act I, Scene 2

[Merry whistling, singing, and good-natured shouting is heard offstage. This entire scene takes place in front of the curtain. Soon Robin appears, stage left, in the company of Will Scarlet and Little John.]

Robin: Will Scarlet, are you certain they are singing these words in the town? That I was naught but a lad of sixteen summers when John Little bested me with his staff?

Scarlet: I assure you, friend Robin, that is exactly what they sing!

Robin: 'Twere better for my reputation if 'twere true. But it says little for Little, here! Why, it makes him into a man who would take on a child! Where's the fairness in that report?

Little John: Oh, but master, they sing not of my age: in truth, I was but a babe of three summers when I bested you! And, to be sure, I used only the hearth-broom!

[All three hoot and laugh at their jesting.]

Robin: Well, my friends, I suppose the folk must have their heroes. And, in the end, it does us and our cause no harm if we are reputed to perform miracles.

Scarlet *[suddenly somber]*: In truth, dear Robin, I sometimes think that the real miracle will occur if our good King Richard does leave his prison and return to these shores.

Robin: Say not "if," Will, but rather, "when." For I have resolved, and the blessed folk of Sherwood have resolved, not to rest until we have raised enough gold to serve as King Richard's ransom and thus return him to his kingdom.

Little John: Resolve as many times as you might wish, Robin. But the truth is that our collections of late have been thin, indeed. It seems as though the only folk traveling through Sherwood are beggars and poor fellows whom the Bishop has robbed

	with his taxes and tools. And, if they were not beggars before, it's certain they feel like beggars when my lord bishop is finished with them.
Scarlet:	True enough! The Bishop puts it out that he amasses funds to ransom our Richard, but I believe him not. He is in Prince John's pocket, mark my words. Why, I believe that every coin he collects will find its way to John.
Little John:	If some portion of those coins do not find their way into the pockets of the Bishop himself....
Robin:	...or into those of our friend, the Sheriff. But hark! Methinks I hear voices in the distance. Will! Creep closer, while John and I hide. Then come tell us who walks the paths of Sherwood this day.

[Will creeps down the riser steps and peers through the "bushes," as the Bishop and Brother Aldric enter from stage right. They continue across the front of the audience and then down the center aisle, talking all the while.]

Brother Aldric:	I understand now why decent, law-abiding folk avoid this forest, my lord.
Bishop:	Ah! Then this is your first venture into Sherwood?
Brother Aldric:	Yes, my lord. And if I have my way, it will be my last. I like not the darkness, the gloom of this place. The thick growth of the trees blocks out all the sun's light. The branches overhead do sway and moan, as if they were spirits let free into the air. Even the birds are strangely silent here.
Bishop:	I agree, dear brother, that Sherwood is a melancholic place. But we must recall that we are men of modern age, of modern mind. And we know that there are no spirits roaming free. Why, next you will be talking of ghosts, man! This is simply a forest of aged trees—the same trees that grow in the copses in our fields, only there are so many of them that it seems darker here, in their midst.
Brother Aldric:	Still, I cannot like this place, though I take much comfort in traveling with such a holy man as yourself. But, my lord, we

have not yet seen any sign of human habitation, nor even any human. Indeed, Sherwood does not seem to be a place of welcome for humankind, though I've no doubt all manner of beasts make their homes here.

Bishop: Brother Aldric, we must never forget that this forest serves as home to many—beasts, yes, but also humans. Some are simple folk, who were born here and would not have any other home. But some are also those who have been driven hence by their own actions—those whom decent folk would do well to avoid. These men have made Sherwood their home by choice, and they live well here, no doubt considering these worrying branches as ample shelter, and killing the royal deer without compunction. *[pause.]*

In fact, Brother Aldric, I think we would be well advised to refer to one another simply as "Brother." I cannot be comfortable in this place if you continue to refer to me as "my lord." We walk together, dressed in the plain brown robes of the mendicant. How then should one of us be "my lord," and the other simply "my brother?"

Brother Aldric: I well understand your meaning, Brother Thomas, and will do my best to follow your direction at all times while we remain in Sherwood.

[They continue down the center aisle, making their way around to the back of the audience. Will Scarlet, having overheard this conversation, creeps silently back to the stage, where Robin and John have been hiding behind bushes, stage left.]

Robin *[beckoning to Will to join him and John in hiding]*: Well, Scarlet, could you discern any travelers of interest?

Scarlet: Indeed, Robin, they are a most interesting company—a company, in fact, of two, who appear to be mendicant friars.

John: Why only appear, Will?

Scarlet: As I listened, I heard one of the brothers, the smaller one, refer to the other as "my lord."

John: Interesting, indeed, as these friars commonly hold to no rank or distinction amongst themselves. But tell me, Will, why you referred to one as "the smaller." Surely begging brothers are generally of the same size?

Scarlet: Indeed, in my experience it is usually so. However, one of these "brothers" was a heavy man, a portly man, a round man—in short, a man whom one could easily imagine dressed in fine robes and presiding at a banquet!

Robin: Hmmm. I have met but few men of such description, and certainly none amongst those who frequent these parts. However.....yes, I suppose it is possible....it so happens that my lord Bishop of Hereford is just such an one!

John: The Bishop? Robin, surely you jest! Why would the Bishop enter Sherwood, and in such a small company, and in such dress?

Robin *[musing]*: Why, indeed?

Scarlet: Robin....

Robin: Yes, friend Will? Do you begin to guess my thinking?

Scarlet: It is possible, I grant you—but is it likely?

John: Ho now! You two would ever hold secrets between you. I do not guess your thinking!

Scarlet: No, John, your strength lies here *[grasping John's upper arm]* and here *[tapping John's shoulders and back]*—but alas, not here *[knocking John's cap off]*!

[They begin a friendly tussle.]

Robin: Here, here, you two! You will make noise enough to wake the dead, and we have serious work to do!

John *[breathlessly]*: But, Robin, I still do not know your meaning!

Robin: Ah, Little John, my friend, let me walk you down that road. Look you, the Bishop of Hereford has been collecting coin

	for Prince John for, lo, these many months, He must by now have amassed a healthy amount of gold. Do you understand me thus far?
John:	Aye. But I still see not how this relates to two friars, carrying their begging bowls through our forest.
Robin:	Only consider, John, that in gaining the gold, he has also gained a conundrum.
John:	Conununun…
Robin:	Exactly. Conundrum. A puzzle, a difficulty, a problem.
John:	But I see no conun….problem in obtaining gold. Is this not what we ourselves aspire to do, to send to King Richard's aid?
Robin:	Indeed. But tell me this: does the Bishop's gold aid Prince John if it remains in Leeds?
John [slowly and thoughtfully]:	Well, no, it does John no good whatsoever. [excitedly, as he has just figured it out] But it does the Bishop good!
Robin:	Yes, but does it do the Bishop good if Prince John has ordered him to collect gold and yet the gold remains in the Bishop's hands?
John [simply]:	Oh, no. Prince John would be very angry.
Scarlet:	Exactly. Therefore, the Bishop's conundrum is…..
John:	How to get the gold safely to Prince John!
Robin:	And there you have it! For what lies between the Bishop and the Prince?
Scarlet:	Why, Sherwood, of course!
John:	And those thieving outlaws-----
All Three:	Robin Hood and his Merry Men!

[A rustling behind the bushes is heard, and Much lifts his head above the greenery.]

Much: Did I hear someone call?

Scarlet: Ho there, Much! You have joined us in right good time, for adventure calls!

Much: Adventure! You know I am ever intrigued by adventure! What obtains?

John: Much! Scarlet, here, has espied two mendicant friars approaching through Sherwood. Know you what this means?

Much: I have seen far too many beggars of late. It means only that they have begged as much as they can in the town, and have been forced to take to the forest in hopes that the Sherwood folk will have food to spare. *[shaking his head]* I fear they will find that our folk are as poor and as starving as the townsfolk.

John: No, no, Much! This means that one of the friars is the Bishop and he carries gold!

Much *[silently gazing at Little John and then slowly shaking his head]*: My friend, I fear you have had too little of the sun, or too much of the shadows, of late. Come, sit down, I will attend to thee, for thou hast always shown me great kindness.

John *[spluttering as Much leads him to a spot and attempts to make him sit]*: What?... thou numbskull!.. Robin! Stop him! *[Robin and Scarlet are convulsed in laughter.]* I say, Robin! Scarlet!... Much! I have no desire to sit! I have no fever!

Robin: Leave him be, Much! He speaks what we believe to be true, only he speaks it too plainly!

Much: But, Robin, why would you think this man is the Bishop? He travels with no guard, no finery, and—on foot, did you say?

Robin: Indeed, I admit that at first glance, it seems to make no sense. This, however, is the very beauty of it. No right-thinking person would believe it possible. Yes, yes... and, unless I mistake me, this was the plan, not of the Bishop, but of the Sheriff! It has the scent of the Sheriff all over it!

Scarlet: And, having the scent of the Sheriff on't, I do agree that the plan makes good sense! So, good my lord, what is our plan? *[Aside to audience]*: And I pray that our plan will make good sense as well!

Robin: Will, you and John and I will proceed along the forest path and waylay these pilgrims. We shall ask for a donation to our fund and see how they respond. Much, do you return to our folk and tell them our plans. Now, silence, my good men, all!

Act I, Scene 3

[Much enters from stage left, carrying a "fire." He looks around stealthily and finally puts it down on the stage, in front of the curtain, about three yards from the side of the stage. He tiptoes back to the entrance and then brings in several "logs" and "rocks," placing them around three sides of the "fire." Brushing his hands together, he surveys his handiwork. Robin, Scarlet, and Little John enter from stage left, dressed awkwardly but clearly as shepherds.]

Much: But what is this I spy? Three shepherds aloose in Sherwood? But, masters all, where be thy sheep?

Little John *[ignoring Much]*: I say, Robin, this wool about my shoulders doth scratch and pull at me until I am like to go mad with the worrying of it!

Scarlet: You complain overmuch, John! Why, Robin is forced to wear a false beard, made of the self-same wool you complain of. And he does not complain!

Robin: Hush, all of you! We will be glad of our subterfuge when the friars arrive, for we must appear to them as simple shepherds. Now, sit. The fire is warm, take up your meat and roast it. Belike our two friends will smell the scent of roasting meat and be drawn, like flies, into our web.

Much: But, Robin, are you certain this disguise will serve? Will they truly think you are here to find lost sheep? After all, sheep do not often wander into Sherwood. At least, not enough to warrant three shepherds searching for them!

Scarlet: Robin, I think friend Much is not as dull as he sometimes seems. There is much to what he says.

Robin: Hmm... Yes, John, take yourself to yonder great tree. Stand you behind it, out of our sight, with your bow at the ready in case our plan goes awry. Much, survey our wood for any other "travelers" this night.

John: And may I take off...?

Robin: Yes, yes, you may take off the wool! We want nothing to interfere with your aim!

[John hastily begins to pull off the wool, leaves and retires to the backstage area, immediately next to the entrance, stage left.]

Robin: Now, Will, no more talk save that of shepherds and sheep. Our flies will soon be upon us, drawn into our pretty trap.

[Bishop and Brother Aldric make their way from the back of the auditorium up the side aisle, stage right. While talking, they gradually approach the stage.]

Brother Aldric: I say, Brother Thomas, I mean not to complain, but my stomach doth growl and moan!

Bishop: Yes, good Brother, we have been traveling now since dawn, and have yet to break our fast. Have you nothing in your pocket that we might nibble upon?

Brother Aldric: Nay, Brother. For the Sheriff was most specific in his orders for our costume. He forbade us to carry or wear anything out of keeping with our disguise. And so I thought, if we are truly beggars, we will have no food to carry with us. And the Sheriff agreed.

Bishop: I'll warrant he agreed most readily. The Sheriff seemed a bit too interested in our costume. Think you that he was perhaps amused by our state?

Brother Aldric [*slyly, all too willing to agree to anything that makes the Sheriff look bad to the Bishop*]: Indeed, the thought did come to mind, Brother, but I hesitated to speak it, as such a thought seemed unworthy of such an ally as the Sheriff has been to us and to our Prince.

Bishop [*sighing*]: Betimes, my Brother, I do fear you are too innocent for the world. A man like the Sheriff can indeed be an ally and a near enemy at the same time. One cannot be too careful with one's choice of friends in this world.

Brother Aldric: Indeed, my lord, I am ever your faithful student in the ways of the world. *[Pause.]* My lord! I think I... Can it be??? Tell me, is that the scent of roasting meat I detect, or is it only my starved belly that plays tricks upon me?

Bishop: Indeed! Then it must be that both our bellies are in a roguish mood, for I also perceive the scent of roasting meat. Belike we are near some forester's hut. Now! Listen well! For, if we are to be with other folk, we must remember who we pretend to be! No more "my lords" now, nor talk of the Sheriff as ally. We are beggars, serving the Lord with our poverty, and ignorant of this place and of the temper of its people. We think only holy thoughts! Mark well my words!

[*By this time, the two are at the front of the auditorium, at the bottom of the risers to the left of center stage. They climb the risers slowly and cautiously, keeping their eyes toward the "fire" and the two men who hover near it, roasting meat upon sticks.*]

Brother Aldric [*in stage whisper*]: See you that fire? And those two fellows? What make you of this cozy scene? They would appear to be shepherds, do you not agree?

Bishop [*in stage whisper*]: Aye, shepherds they do appear to be. But be on your guard, Brother. Things are not always as they seem. These two could even be outlaws in disguise—watch your tongue, and be prepared to use your staff if the need arises.

Brother Aldric: Indeed, we are fortunate that there are but two of them—a match for the two of us if it comes to that!

Bishop: Greetings, and blessings upon thee, neighbors!

Scarlet [*looking up as if startled, dropping his meat and jumping to his feet immediately, grasping his staff with both hands in a defensive pose*]: What!??! Who goes there? I know of no "neighbors" in this part of Sherwood! Why say you "neighbors?" Who goes there? [*peering into the "gloom"*]

Bishop: Fear not, my good man! For we are only two, and two seeking the generosity of the forest—much like you yourselves, I dare say. We have walked far this day, and have met no one save yourselves upon the road. We are only humble friars, accepting from the world what it has to offer, and sending our gratitude on to heaven.

Scarlet: Hmmph. You would do well to take care of "what the world has to offer," Brothers, if you would keep your heads and your freedom. These woods, they do say, shelter many who have fled civil society and watch the paths to catch the unwary in their snares.

Bishop: We have no fears of such, fellow, for we are but simple friars, begging for the very food we eat. We carry naught but our bowls and our staves.

Brother Aldric [*who has been staring fixedly at the meat, inching closer and closer to the fire*]: I say, friends, for you do appear to be friends, have you sustenance to spare for two weary travelers? We have walked far, and have yet to break our fast.

Scarlet [*looking at the meat and at Robin, who shrugs his shoulders and hands two sticks, bearing meat already roasted, up to Will*]: I grant you, we had intended to sup on this meat at moonrise. But your need, it seems is greater than ours, and we will no doubt find our supper in good time. For, as you say, the forest is generous.

[*The two "friars" each take a stick of meat and sit at the fire, hungrily gnawing at the meat. For a few moments no one speaks, as they all eat.'*]

Brother Aldric: But tell me, good men, how came you to Sherwood? You have the look of country folk—do you make your home nearby?

Scarlet: Nay, we are but shepherds seeking stray sheep within the wood.

Brother Aldric: Do many stray? I like not this forest, and would not want to come here overmuch.

Scarlet: Not many stray, but enough to keep us busy. Today we seek two. *[Robin coughs, as if choking.]* Here, here, my friend! *[patting him on the back]* Have a draught of water, there's a good fellow!

Bishop: Your friend has been strangely silent throughout our greetings and our meal. Is this a common state with him?

Robin: Nay, good friar, I can speak well enough when I have ought to say.

Bishop: Hah! He does speak! And what have you to say, good fellow?

Robin: I have been pondering your payment for the good meat you have taken from our hands.

Bishop: Payment? Look at us, man—what payment could such as we offer? We carry naught but our bowls and our staves!

Robin: You mistake my meaning, good Brother! We are simple folk who stray not far from the forest. And so, for entertainment, we must depend on ourselves. You have lately been in the town—know you any ballad, or play, or merry tune? For we do like music after a meal, and we grow weary of our own devices.

Brother Aldric: Ah, now I see your meaning. But, alas, we have neither voice nor lute with which to pass the time. And, being holy men, we know only holy stories, and those we know only in Latin.

Scarlet: But this is too sad! You have no gold, you have no music, you have no tales!

Robin: And yet, my friends, you each have two feet.

Bishop: Two feet? Why, so do all whole men.

Scarlet *[to Robin]*: Hah! He makes a jest! They are holy men who are also whole men!

Robin: You find jests in almost any word, fellow! But my meaning is rather this: Let them dance for their meal!

Scarlet: Dance? Why, yes! It is the very thing! A merry jig would raise our spirits and settle our stomachs!

Brother Aldric: Surely you both are jesting now? Surely you cannot expect two churchmen to dance?

Scarlet: Oh, come now, Sirrah! You have traveled far. Surely you have wandered through towns on market days and have witnessed lads and lasses in their merry leaps and twirls. And I wager, you have tapped your very toes, wishing to forsake your vows and join in the jollity!

Robin: Yes! And here is your opportunity! There is no one to see you save simple shepherds. Dance, my friends, dance!

Brother Aldric *[looking at the Bishop warily]*: Very well, I will oblige you. But Brother Thomas carries too much weight to be comfortable leaping about.

Robin: He carries too much weight, does he? But I know of a friar hereabouts who carries even more weight than our worthy brother here, and he dances whenever the pipes begin to play! Up, up, you two, and offer us a jig!

Brother Aldric: No, no, upon my word, we cannot!

Robin: Yes, yes, upon my word, you shall!

Bishop: Upon my word, there has been enough nonsense. We thank you most heartily for sharing with us your meat, good fellows. Aand now we leave you to find your sheep. Accept our blessings as payment for your kindness.

Robin: A dance I have called for, and a dance I shall have. But perhaps we have not provided a proper incentive, having no music to offer. I know of one nearby who can offer music aplenty. John!

[John steps from behind the tree, bow at the ready.]

John: Yes, Master?

Robin: John, our two friars here have taken our meat, and yet they refuse us a dance. What say you to this? I fear we have no music to give their feet the proper rhythm.

John: Master! I know the very thing! Only allow me to loose my arrows in sprightly measure *[aiming his bow at their feet]*, and the twang of the bow and the thump of the arrow will provide a proper rhythm, indeed! *[He pulls back and prepares to loose an arrow.]*

Robin: A right good noggin you do have, John Little! We shall have drum, and pipe, and dance!

[The Bishop and Brother Aldric, looking at one another in dismay, begin to shuffle their feet.]

Scarlet: Come, come now, friends! If you can lift your heels no higher than that, we must think of further incentive!

[The Bishop and Brother Aldric begin to dance with more energy. Robin, Scarlet, and John laugh heartily, Robin and Scarlet clapping their hands. But as the two "friars" jump higher and twirl about, a sound of jingling is distinctly heard.]

Robin: Hold! Drum and pipe I did expect—but from whence comes the tambourine? How is it, brothers, that you should have such worldly instruments within your robes?

Bishop: No, no, you mistake the sound. We have no tambourines about us, I assure you!

Brother Aldric: Tambourines? I never go near the things! They are not made for sacred music! I make only holy tunes!

Robin: No? Leap a little more, my fine friends, and take care to open your ears.

[As John has aimed his bow directly at their feet, and has no smile upon his face, the two "friars" leap tentatively. The jingling sound is clear, once more.]

Robin: You see, my friends—there it is again! I have a hankering to see these tambourines you say you do not carry beneath your robes. For, bless me, their jingle and jangle is the sweetest I have heard—it is a silver sound, a golden sound, a sound to warm the heart. And I would have these tambourines for my very own! Lift your robes!

[The "friars" reluctantly and awkwardly lift the backs of their robes and take out the bags of gold.]

Scarlet: But what is this? John, keep your bow steady! For I think me that these bags are filled with coin!

Robin: Yes, truly we heard sounds of silver and gold! And, if I be not mistaken, these are not two plain friars we have before us. Gentlemen, may I introduce His Grace, the Bishop of Hereford and his clerk, Brother Aldric?

Bishop *[recognizing Robin as he removes his beard]*: And—can it be? Heaven protect us! For it is the rogue himself—Robin Hood!

Robin *[sweeping a bow]*: Yes, Your Grace. Though I know it is only proper manners for me to reply with "at your service," I, in fact, serve another—King Richard by name. But I shall serve you nonetheless. For I believe this is the very treasure you have been accumulating in Leeds to send as ransom for our King. I shall serve your purpose by ensuring that it is sent to Germany as promised. One must take care whom one trusts, Your Grace. I do not trust Prince John and his allies to send the ransom for the King.

Bishop *[with a stern voice]*: You shall live to regret this day, Robert of Locksley.

Robin: Oh, I think not, Your Grace. Those who do good in this world have no regrets. Perhaps you would do well to remember that yourself.

John: All this "tit for tat" is well and good, Robin, but how shall we leave our merry guests, or shall we see them on their way?

Robin: I think.....yes! I think we shall leave our guests as they would have had us believe them to be—bound to one another in holy vows of poverty! Scarlet, take this cord and bind them, back to back! Then let them find their own way out of this most generous forest *[holding up the bags of coins and jingling them]*!

[Scarlet binds them as Robin pantomimes putting out the fire, and John continues to keep watch with drawn bow. All three outlaws enjoy the spectacle immensely. When Scarlet is done, they all three sweep bows to the two "friars" and, laughing merrily, run off, stage left. The two "friars" make their way, with great difficulty, stumbling and falling over each other offstage, behind the curtain, stage right. Much returns from stage left to clear the stage of the "fire," etc.]

Act II, Scene 1

[The Bishop and Brother Aldric, still bound together, stumble out from behind the curtain, stage right.]

Bishop *[huffing and puffing]*: I say, Brother, must you tend so much toward your own direction? We will make more progress if we both move in the same path.

Brother Aldric *[also huffing and puffing, and irritated but trying not to appear so]*: My observation, as well, my lord Bishop. I attempt to remain on the path, whilst it seems as if you would tend ever toward the undergrowth!

Bishop: That makes no sense, Brother. I have no desire to become entangled in the shrubbery! It is you who pulls ever toward the trees on your side!

Brother Aldric: Nay, my lord, nay! For have I not said how I detest the darkness of this forest? It is thee, thyself, whom I attempt to follow. Indeed, thou art so much heavier than I, that I have no choice but to follow!

Bishop: I beg your pardon, my lord clerk. Indeed, my lord puny clerk! I would caution thee to remember thy station!

Brother Aldric *[realizing his misstep]*: Oh! My lord Bishop! Pray forgive me! I am so overwrought at our position, and at the difficulty of maintaining uprightness and dignity when bound thus together, that I do forget myself! Pray believe that I meant no harm or criticism!

[By this time the two are to the left of center stage. Both are gazing with large eyes upon the sight of the risers before them.]

Bishop *[slowly]*: And now, my lord intelligent, trustworthy clerk, tell me this: How shall we maintain uprightness and dignity whilst negotiating this steepy hill?

Brother Aldric *[opens his mouth to reply]*: Alas! Regrettably, my lord...

[At this moment, a fumbling and stumbling is heard behind the curtain, stage right, and the Sheriff and his Sergeant appear with drawn swords, breathless as if they have been running.]

Sheriff: Halt! Who goes there?

Sergeant: Who rows there?

[The Bishop and Brother Aldric pivot their heads so they can look at one another, then pivot their heads in the opposite direction to look behind them at the approaching men.]

Bishop and Brother Aldric *[simultaneously]*: Who goes where?

Sheriff and Sergeant *[simultaneously]*: Who rows there?

[Bishop and Brother Aldric pivot their heads back to look at one another.]

Brother Aldric: Can it be that he does not recognize the results of his own disguises?

Bishop: No, no, this cannot be!

[They pivot their heads back to look at the officers.]

Bishop: My lord Sheriff! Can it be that you do not recognize the results of your own disguises?

Sheriff: What mean you, man? We seek the outlaw, Robin Hood!

Sergeant: We see the in-law, Robin Hood!

[At these words, Robin, John, and Scarlet creep onstage from stage left and hide among the bushes there. As the scene unfolds, they greatly enjoy the spectacle.]

Bishop: Come closer, man, and look on our faces.

Sheriff: How can I be assured that you are not armed, that this is not some ruse?

Sergeant: Yes, how can we know that this is no noose?

Brother Aldric: Look you at our hands and arms, man! What weapon could we fit amongst these bonds?

[They make a great show of turning all the way around so that the officers can see their hands and arms, bound on both sides.]

Sheriff: It is true, you seem to be unarmed.

Sergeant: Yes, you mean no harm.

Sheriff: Sergeant, I forbid you to repeat my words!

Sergeant: Yes, Sir! I shall not repeat your words!

Sheriff: But you do repeat my words!

Sergeant: Not, so, my lord Sheriff. If you would attend, you would be able to distermine that I repeat not your very words, but rather the sense of them. For I have learned in life that it is best not to dispute the unmentions of one's employer.

Sheriff *[beginning to steam with irritation]*: Sergeant! If you wish to remain in the employ of this employer, you will speak your own thoughts, or you will not speak at all. Is this clear?

Sergeant: Yes, Sir! I will not squeak or call!

Sheriff *[turning red with frustration]*: Now that we have established that you are unarmed, perhaps you would do us the very great favor of stating your names and your business here in Sherwood.

Bishop *[in dangerously threatening tones]*: My lord Sheriff, as the person whom I hold responsible for both my current name and my current occupation, I would advise you to tread carefully here!

Sheriff *[aghast, as he has come closer to peer into their faces]*: My lord Bishop of Hereford! Brother Aldric!

Bishop: Indeed. And, as I have no other choice at the moment, I am—at your service.

Sheriff: My lord! How came you to be in such circumstance?

Bishop: It was as we feared. That scoundrel, Robin Hood, took us in with his disguise and stole all the money from us.

Brother Aldric: Yes, he and one of his men were dressed as shepherds. They offered us food which we accepted as we had not broken fast since rising this morning and *[as the Sheriff looks about to speak]*... How were we to know they were outlaws?

[The Sergeant spots the men hiding in the bushes, and begins to watch them closely.]

Sheriff: They offered you meat?

Brother Aldric: Yes, and I must say the venison was quite tasty, though it came from an outlaw's fire.

[The Sergeant realizes that the hiding men are the outlaws. He starts to speak, but remembers that he has promised not to speak. He claps his hands over his mouth, as his eyes get bigger and bigger.]

Sheriff: Venison? How do you suppose he came to offer venison?

Bishop: But, Sirrah—surely you cannot mean...?

Sheriff: Indeed I do mean! He has fed you of the King's own deer!

Brother Aldric: Well, if it was the King's own deer, in truth we paid dearly for it! For, after we had eaten, they demanded payment, and we...

Bishop *[quickly interrupting]*: ... And as they had discovered that we carried the gold, they took it all!

[At this point, the Sergeant can scarcely contain himself. He begins to shake and quiver in place, and catches the attention of the Bishop.]

Bishop: I say, Sheriff, does your sergeant suffer from the tremors? If so, he should surely take himself to his bed and leave the company of healthy men.

Sheriff: My ser— *[turning to look at the man]* ...indeed, what ails thee, man?

[The Sergeant, keeping one hand over his mouth, points feebly toward the bushes.]

Sheriff: What is all this jittering and pointing? Speak, man, speak!

[Robin and his men, seeing the sergeant point, rapidly and quietly creep behind the curtain.]

Sergeant *[with great relief]*: Ah, thank you, your lordship, indeed I am believed to be allowed to speak after all this time of silence!

Sheriff *[exasperated]*: Never mind all that! What have you to say?

Sergeant: Sir, as you and yonder holy men stood conversating, I observed Robin Hood and members of his band in yonder shrubbery.

Sheriff: You saw... and you did not speak?

Sergeant: No, my lord, for you very specificously instructed me not to speak, as I had no words of my own, and I never have words of my own, my lord, as I always lie down upon the wisdom of others to fill my mouth.

Sheriff *[turning red again, and in a threatening tone]*: Upon my oath as sheriff, when we return to Nottingham, I shall.....

Bishop *[in an exaggeratedly bored voice]*: My lord Sheriff, might I recall you to the present situation? We have strong evidence that the outlaws we seek are yet in this vicinity, and I—and of course, my clerk—are yet bound one to the other. Might I be so bold as to suggest that you leave your difficulties with your employees for our arrival in Nottingham, and that you spend the next few moments removing our bonds?

Sheriff: Of course, my lord Bishop. I have been remiss. Sergeant, do you take the other side whilst I take this one, and we shall remove these bonds post haste.

[As they work on the ropes, the Sheriff gives his orders.]

Sheriff: My lord Bishop: our horses are hidden in the trees but a short way through the forest there. Sergeant, you will lead my lord Bishop to the horses, and the two of you will proceed with all due haste to Nottingham, where you will sound the alarm and direct my best bowmen to find and attend to us here in Sherwood. My good Brother Aldric, you and I will search these woods round about and try to discover the hiding place of these outlaws. *[The ropes are undone.]* Now, off with you, and, Sergeant, the path lies straight ahead. Try not to get lost.

Sergeant: Yes, Your Honorship, I will try to get lost.

Bishop *[as Sheriff rolls his eyes heavenward in what appears to be a silent prayer for patience]*: To be sure, I shall be glad to depend upon four legs instead of these two for the remainder of my journey to Nottingham. Brother Aldric, see that you comport yourself as is worthy of my most trusted clerk.

[The Bishop and the Sergeant exit, stage right. Brother Aldric watches them depart, with his mouth open in dismay.]

Brother Aldric: But... but... I loathe this forest!

Sheriff *[clapping him on the shoulder]*: Come now, Brother! Here is our plan. My Sergeant pointed in that direction, so we shall proceed, looking for signs of the outlaws' passing. And when we find them, we shall lie in hiding until my archers find us. Of course, it is always possible that the outlaws will find us before we find them. In that case, you'll have the opportunity to truly earn your Bishop's trust! Let's see what kind of a man you really are! Surely, you do not mean to spend all your days indoors, counting gold and wondering what's for dinner? How are you with a sword? No? The bow? But we must cease this idle chatter. We must go through the forest as if we were forest creatures ourselves. I do believe there are wolves hereabouts! Let us pretend we are wolves, Brother!

[The Sheriff is obviously having fun at the expense of the terrified Brother Aldric, who is, in fact, so terrified that he cannot speak. They make their way down the risers and exit, stage left.]

Act II, Scene 2

[Robin arrives breathlessly from stage right. He looks around furtively, and creeps up the risers to center stage.]

Robin *[breathlessly]*: That foul Sheriff follows too closely for this outlaw's comfort! Mayhap I shall find shelter in this cottage!

[Robin knocks on the "door of the cottage." An Old Woman parts the curtain and peers up into Robin's face.]

Old Woman: Eh, eh? Who is't knocks at old Leticia's door? Why—if I be not mistaken, 'tis Robert Locksley? Eh?

Robin: Yes, yes, Mother Leticia, 'tis Robert indeed! I have fair memories of your cakes and sweets from my youth.

Old Woman: And now I hear you have become outlaw, and they call you "Robin Hood."

Robin: Yes, good Mother, but I am only outlawed until our rightful king, Richard, returns. And, good Mother, I fear I come to you in dire need of help. For the Sheriff of Nottingham is fast on my heels, and should he catch me, 'tis the gallows for sure!

Old Woman: Then come, come! Stand not at the door a-gabbling as do the geese!

[The curtains open part-way to reveal the interior of a poor cottage. There are a hearth with an iron pot over the feeble fire, a rough table, a rough shelf, two stools, and a cupboard.]

Old Woman: Now, what is your plan, good Robert? —For I remember well my young Robin, and, as a youth, you always had a plan!

Robin: To be sure, Mother! But here I have not the time for one of my more worthy schemes. Only...have you another skirt and apron, Mother, that I might disguise myself as you?

Old Woman [*cackling*]: Indeed, good Robin! Now watch you well how I move when I search for them in my cupboard! Takes skill to appear to be aged, upon my faith, it does!

[She opens the cupboard door, rummages around, finds a shift, a skirt, an apron, and a shawl.]

Old Woman: Here, Robin, the skirt, first of all, then the apron, and last, the shawl about thy head. And take good care to cover thy face well! For thy face, alas, is the face of youth!

Robin [*dressing hastily and clumsily*]: Oh, Mother Leticia, I am ever in thy debt!

Old Woman: But what shall you do with me? All the folk know that only one old woman abides in this cot.

Robin [*pausing a moment and looking around*]: I would have thee out of the way of danger, Mother. Therefore, we shall hide thee in this cupboard here. Now, listen carefully, Mother. You must not make one sound—save, from time to time, I would have thee moan, as one in great pain, or perhaps as a wandering spirit. Can you make such a sound?

Old Woman [*cackling*]: Indeed, my Robert, I am no stranger to such moans!

[She climbs into the cupboard and Robin closes the door carefully. He takes up the hearth broom and makes a great business of sweeping the hearth and tending to the fire. The Sheriff and Brother Aldric run quietly through the stage right entrance and creep up the risers. They stop on the top riser, as they see the cottage before them.]

Brother Aldric [*breathlessly*]: Look—a dwelling! Perhaps they will have food and drink! I am near to perishing for hunger and thirst!

Sheriff [*scornfully*]: You and your belly and your constant whining! Perhaps those within will have seen or heard the outlaws nearby.

[They approach the "door" and the Sheriff "knocks," not waiting for a response before he throws open the door. The "Old Woman" has continued to sweep and fuss about the hearth while the two men have been talking.]

Sheriff *[loudly and in a commanding voice]*: Good woman! I say, good woman!

["She" turns around slowly.]

Old Woman: Eh? Good even, gentlemen. What is your business in these parts, and what is your business with old Leticia? Eh?

Sheriff: Good Woman, I am the Sheriff of Nottingham and this is my—er—companion. We seek outlaws who have lately been seen nearby. Know you aught of the scoundrel called "Robin Hood" and his band?

Old Woman: Aye, Leticia hears of outlaws from time to time.

Brother Aldric: And have you any food or drink, for we are like to faint from hunger.

Sheriff: Be quiet, you fool! Your belly is the least of our business. Has anyone unknown to you been near this cottage this day?

Old Woman *[sighing]*: Nay, nay. Folk have forgotten about poor old Leticia. But there was a time, in my youth, when...

Brother Aldric: We have no business with your youth, woman, but only with today.

[A frail moan is heard in the background.]

Brother Aldric: But... but... what is that sound I hear?

Old Woman: What sound do you hear, brother, for I hear naught.

Brother Aldric: That... that sound so like a moan!

Old Woman: Moan, you say? Ah! To be sure, that 'twould be our Spirit! But take you no mind of her. I am certain she would not harm such gentlemen as yourselves.

Sheriff: Harm? What mean you by this "harm?"

Old Woman: 'Tis just an old tale told in these parts that, when her moan is heard, then someone who hears it is like to die. But take no notice of it, take no notice.

Brother Aldric: Take no notice! How can you say so? And have I not said from the start of my journey into this forest that it was accursed? *[The moan sounds again.]* Let us leave this place!

Sheriff *[patting Brother Aldric on the shoulder]*: Now, now, good Brother! Surely 'tis only the wind through the boughs! Let us sit here awhile and partake of the good mother's hospitality! What of your hunger? What of your thirst? Sit! Sit! And, perhaps, as she serves us, the good woman will tell us what she knows of Robin Hood and his men. Have you aught to eat, woman?

Old Woman: Eat? Well, perchance there is a loaf of bread on my hearth. But for drink, you must take you to the brook nearby.

[She places a loaf of dark bread on the table, strongly enough that it can be heard to "thump" by the audience.]

Brother Aldric *[taking out a knife and attempting to cut into the bread]*: In truth, if this bread were harder, 'twould be a veritable stone!

Sheriff: You have grown soft with your counting and your sitting, Brother. Let me show you how to cut a loaf!

[He takes out his sword and cuts the loaf in two.]

Sheriff: There, Brother, eat 'til you are filled.

[The two attempt to break off bits of the bread and chew. The "spirit" moans again. Brother Aldric puts down his bread and gazes fearfully at the cupboard. The Sheriff picks up Brother Aldric's bread and firmly places it back in his hand.]

Brother Aldric *[timidly]*: I say, this bread is hard. Have you no meat, mother?

Sheriff *[fixing his eye upon Brother Aldric]*: Yes, mother, have you no venison, perchance, in that cupboard of yours?

Old Woman: Venison, you say? Good Sheriff, surely you know the King's law: that all game within Sherwood is the King's own. Old Leticia would not eat the King's deer.

Sheriff: Nonetheless, I would see within that cupboard. For if you do have venison, it says to me that you have friends whom I would perchance like to meet!

[He walks pointedly toward the cupboard as the Old Woman backs toward the hearth. As he opens the cupboard door, Robin blows upon his horn and takes up his sword, throwing back his head and tearing off his shawl.]

Robin: Close enough, my friend, close enough: For there is treasure within that cupboard worth more to me than any venison!

Sheriff: There is within only one small aged woman! Or have you hid the King's gold within as well?

Robin: In truth, one aged woman is worth more to me than all the King's gold—a sentiment you, I daresay, would not understand! But let me assure you that the King's gold is, at this very moment, on its way to Germany. You, yourself, will have to explain the whereabouts of the gold that the Prince no doubt expects.

Sheriff *[drawing his sword]*: Thou scoundrel! Thou rogue! I shall have thy head for this!

[The Old Woman peers around the cupboard door from time to time. Brother Aldric edges backward nearer and nearer to the cottage door. Little John and Will Scarlet rush quietly from stage left. They arrive at the door of the cottage just as the Sheriff draws his sword. They stand quietly, awaiting orders from Robin.]

Robin: I'll have that sword for safekeeping, my lord Sheriff, for I believe thou art outnumbered, and I care not for an unfair fight.

[The Sheriff looks around and sees Scarlet and John and looks back toward Robin as the Old Woman takes up the hearth broom as if it were a staff. He throws down his sword scornfully. Scarlet and John motion to Brother Aldric to join the Sheriff.]

Sheriff: You'll regret this day, Robert Locksley, you and all your men. For, mark my words, Richard shall die in his prison and John shall be King.

Robin: I would not worry overmuch about other men's fates, my lord Sheriff. It is your own fate should concern you at the moment.

[The Sheriff looks around the room, at Robin and his men and their weapons, silently.]

Little John: What shall it be, Robin? The sword or the bow?

Robin *[musingly]*: Neither, I think, John... Nay, first let us blindfold them and lead them from this place. *[Scarlet and John take out cloth and begin to blindfold the Sheriff and Brother Aldric.]* I daresay neither of them could find their way out of Sherwood if their lives depended upon it—which is, in fact, the truth of the matter. And then....yes, the very thing! Will, are we still in possession of those two donkeys who—er—wandered into our hands but one month past?

Will: Yes, Master, and they are the fatter for having been in our care.

Robin: Good! Good! We shall take these fine fellows and bind them to the donkeys and send them trotting along into Nottingham. In such wise, both the donkeys and the men shall find themselves once more at home.

Old Woman: A right good plan, young Robin! But—you would not want them to forget Sherwood too soon, would you?

Robin *[looking at her with amusement]*: Of course not, Mother Leticia! You are quite correct!

Scarlet: Indeed! The perfect ending to a most perfect adventure!

Little John *[complaining and confused]*: What? What ending? I listen to every word but still I do not understand!

Old Woman: Never mind, good John, I have venison within the cupboard and ale in the spring, and I have saved them all for my strong protector.

Little John: But, Grandmother, what mean they by this "ending"?

Old Woman: My John, they mean only this: that you shall bind these two on the tops of the donkeys. But so they will not soon forget Sherwood's hospitality, they shall be bound backwards, so they might face toward our forest whilst they trot toward the town!

Little John *[as he helps Scarlet bind the hands of the two men, while Robin watches over them with drawn sword]*: But, Grandmother! This is indeed the perfect ending! For they shall watch the ends of the donkeys, all the way home!

[Little John joins Robin and Scarlet as they escort the Sheriff and Brother Aldric out of the "cottage door" and off stage right. Mother Leticia watches them fondly, and then goes back to her sweeping as the curtain closes.]

FINIS

The Philosopher's Stone

Characters: Celia Simple   Gilbert Gullible
             Catherine Catchall   William Worthy
             Master Duplicitous   Celia's Mother
             Duchess of Dishawash   Watchman [no police until 1833]

Prologue

A parade of characters enters from stage right and begins to traverse the front of the auditorium, up the stage stairs, across the stage, down the opposite stairs, and exit stage left.

First Grouping: *Duchess, Catherine, and Watchman. They walk in order, the Duchess followed by Catherine and then the Watchman [dressed as a common porter], carrying various boxes and parcels. The Duchess speaks with her nose in the air and seeming to look over the head of whomever she is addressing. Using the "first person plural"—the "royal 'we'"—it must be clear that she is referring only to herself.*

Duchess *[to Catherine]*: Our position, my dear, in society,
    Is one of sober propriety.
    Though our heart be light, we never laugh;
    Nor do our features reveal our wrath.
    No errant smile, no affecting tear
    Shall disarrange our haughty sneer.
    For we, my child, are nobility,
    And we model good manners for all to see.
    We are, for common folk, a strong recourse
    When judgment and wisdom they seek perforce.

Catherine: I am indeed overwhelmed, Your Grace,
That my education you do undertake.
For my family is common to the core,
My father a merchant who minds a store!

Duchess: Ah, my dear, 'twas your intelligent face
That caught our attention in a crowded space.
As we sit in state in our great hall
And ponder the cases that before us fall,
Intelligence sparks good judgment, we find;
Nothing so inspires as a lively mind.

Catherine: Your Grace, you do me great honor indeed.
I shall endeavor to meet your every need.

Watchman: Aargh! *[He begins to drop parcels, having been staggering under their weight, clearly burdened from the time he entered the auditorium.]*

Duchess: Indeed, my child, then perhaps you might strive
To relieve this fellow of parcels, er, one through five.

[The Duchess continues across to exit, leaving Catherine and Watchman to struggle with the parcels, which they do with gusto: stacking them up and trying to catch them as they fall, several times, until they finally balance them.]

Watchman: I say, Mistress Catchall, I know not how
You can bear to be in the presence of that old cow!

Catherine: Guard your tongue! It is broad day!
And remember your duty here, I pray!

Watchman *[sitting and wiping his brow]*:
Oh, yes, my duty, now let me call it up...
I am to search for signs of a miserable cup!

Catherine: NOT a "miserable cup," indeed!
But the venerable Chalice of St. Mary Mead!
Remember you, 'twas the very container
That William the Conqueror gave to his retainer.
And that self-same fellow had the honor to be
The ancestor of our Duchess—yes, SHE!

> *[pointing toward the Duchess]*
> Ah me, what a state of affairs, to be sure.
> The cup's been stolen. It's not to be endured!

[Catherine and Watchman, sighing heavily, pick up the parcels and trudge off in the wake of the Duchess.]

Second Grouping *enters as First Group exits: Gilbert and William. They are deep in conversation.*

Gilbert: Ah, my friend, I think and think,
But all my little thoughts then seem to sink
In a soup of thoughts—and none of them bubbles
Into the answer that would ease my troubles!

William *[looking out at the audience, rolling his eyes, and shrugging his shoulders]*:
Gilbert, you know you are my very best friend—
Seeing you unhappy causes my heart to rend.
Can you not a little insight share,
That I might know what brings you such care?

Gilbert: William, in truth, we've been friends since birth...
Yes, I'll tell you what's robbed me of my mirth!
In my workshop I now toil daily,
For I, who was used to live so gaily,
Have devoted my youth to a marvelous quest
That's puzzled scholars from east to west!
And now you understand why I seem so distracted,
Why my thoughts take flight, why my heart's impacted!

William *[scratching his head]*:
Um...dear Gilbert... pray forgive my unwitting density,
But I fail to understand the source of your intensity!

Gilbert: My friend, I know you as one who's discreet—
[excitedly, with agitation]
I seek to achieve a most unusual feat;
The Philosopher's Stone I seek to unmask!
This is my joy, my passion, my task!

42

William *[looking at the audience, shocked and dismayed]*:
    Gilbert, dear friend, my own heart's twin!
    What nonsense have you now got caught up in?
    The Philosopher's Stone! Why, everyone knows
    That's a waste of time, a ridiculous hoax!

Gilbert *[hurt and miffed]*:
    Well, of course, if you think that I
    Would engage in a hoax, a spurious lie—
    William, you hurt me to the quick!
    I cannot think! My heart is sick!

William: Oh, Gilbert! Please wait! I meant no offense!
    My surprise and my ignorance have made me dense!
    Please! Explain to me further your so serious quest;
    I'll listen, I promise! We'll put your hurt to rest!

[William and Gilbert hurry off toward the stage left exit, William attempting to comfort Gilbert and restore himself to his good graces, Gilbert having none of it.]

Third Grouping: *Celia with her Mother. They are arguing.*

Mother: But I am only concerned about your welfare, my love!
    Come, be a good girl, be my own little dove!
    Child, if you consider it, you must agree
    That your betrothed is strange. He is not ordinary!

Celia: Exactly! Gilbert is far from ordinary!
    But he is not strange, and he is not scary!
    He is sensitive, imaginative, and kind—
    His heart is of gold, of quicksilver his mind!

Mother: Child, child, you know naught of the world.
    This boy has put your head in a whirl!
    Listen to your mother, I've seen this before—
    He's losing his mind—it's this quest he adores!
    He'll work and work 'til your heart's naught but rubble,
    And before it's all over—you'll both be in trouble!
    My dearest daughter, put marriage aside!!
    I'll find you a handsome new husband betide.

Celia [*running toward the stage left exit*]:
>No! No! A thousand times, no!
>He has my heart, to him I will go!

Fourth Grouping: *Gilbert steps out from behind the curtain, stage left. Master Duplicitous steps out from behind the curtain, stage right. He crouches, hiding from Gilbert.*

Gilbert [*triumphantly and dreamily*]:
>I am close, I am close, I feel it in my bones!
>One day soon I'll find the Philosopher's Stone!
>And then I'll have gold, enough to repair
>All the world's woes, all the world's cares.

[*He moves back behind the curtain.*]

Master Duplicitous [*mockingly*]:
>You are close, you are close, what a silly bones!
>And you think you'll find the Philosopher's Stone!
>I'll find gold in a way tried and true,
>By taking advantage of fools like you!

ACT I, Scene 1

The curtain opens to reveal the Duchess interrogating the Watchman. The Watchman is dressed more formally than in the previous scene. She sits in her raised seat [almost a throne]. He stands before her.

Duchess: And now, my good man, you will report to us all that you have discovered. When shall we expect the return of our family's treasured chalice?

Watchman [*gracefully bowing*]: Your Grace, my cohorts and I have blanketed the town, the shire, indeed the entire countryside and the Continent besides! We shall leave no stone unturned, no squirrel undisturbed, no wildflower unquestioned, no hearth unswept...

Duchess: Stop! We are out of all patience with your flowers and squirrels! Tell us straight away! Where is our cup?

Watchman *[gracefully bowing]*: Your Grace is naturally perturbed at the loss of such an important family vessel. Why, who knows, the lips of Duke William himself did likely lick the lead of its lining! His fingers fondled its flowing frame. *[His fingers twist and turn deliberately.]* His eye beheld its beveled beauty…

Duchess *[with barely contained antagonism]*: Good Watchman, if you do not cease this ridiculous prattle and respond to our query at once, we shall call our guards and have you placed in our dampest and draftiest dungeon, where you shall no doubt discourse with the dancing drops of dew drifting dreadfully down to the dysfunctional and noticeably dirty ditch! Do you understand us?

Watchman *[gracefully bowing]*: Yes, Your Grace. Of a certainty, Your Grace.

Duchess: Then answer us!

Watchman: Yes, Your Grace. Without delay, Your Grace. The facts, as they now stand, indicate that your chalice has not yet come to light.

Duchess: We take it that the chalice remains at large, undiscovered, and lost?

Watchman: Yes, Your Grace, despite all our efforts.

Duchess: And your plan?

Watchman: Our plan for proceeding, Your Grace, is a plump and perspicacious program. *[He takes out a large magnifying glass and does an exaggerated "tip-toe" around her apartment.]* We shall apprehend the cup and the perfidious pickpocket who plucked it from its rightful place in your palace. We shall…

Duchess: Enough! In other words, you have no plan! Well then, attend closely to ours! You shall assign all your troop to discovering our chalice, and you shall report your progress to us daily, if not hourly. Is this clear? And, if we are forced to send our staff in search of you in order to apprehend your report, it shall not go well with you, do you understand?

Watchman [*Momentarily stunned, he recovers and gracefully bows as he backs out of the room.*]: Yes, Your Grace. Of a certainty, Your Grace. Without fail, Your Grace…

The curtain closes.

ACT I, Scene 2

Catherine and William walk onto the stage, in front of the curtain.

Catherine [*worried*]: But, William, are you certain you heard him correctly? Gilbert has always seemed a bit of the innocent, but I have never thought him foolish!

William: Yes, I, too, have thought him naïve. But I have always attributed this to his kind heart. He is totally unwilling to think that anyone would want to take advantage of him, or have ulterior motive. I assure you, I heard him correctly. He is trying to discover the secret of the Philosopher's Stone.

Catherine: "Philosopher's Stone"… Is this not the supposed alchemical substance which, when discovered, is reputed to enable its owner to turn any base metal—or at least, lead—into gold?

William: Yes. It has been the subject of innumerable treatises and conjectures, by the most learned of men. But we are people of true science now, and everyone knows that all those treatises are pure poppycock! Everyone, that is, except our friend, Gilbert Gullible.

Catherine: Yes, dear boy that he is. And, by extension, I suppose that my lifelong friend Celia Simple, to whom he has been affianced since infancy, also believes this nonsense. Anything Gilbert says has the force of an eternal truth in her mind! [*She sighs loudly.*] Oh, William, what are we to do?

William:	I can think of nothing to do, save watch over the two of them and thus attempt to protect them from themselves.
Catherine:	Yes, at all costs we must maintain our friendship with them. We must do nothing which might cause them to spurn our affections, else they will indeed be entirely without protection.
William:	I fear you are correct, my dear. For, if they are dabbling about in alchemy, their innocence will prove no defense against the perfidy of others.
Catherine:	As our first strategy, friend William, I suggest that I visit Celia this very afternoon. Perhaps her mother can be of some assistance.
William:	I'll warrant you are correct, dear Catherine. I, on the other hand, will make my way 'round to Gilbert's lodging. He appears to be spending his entire allowance on equipment for this spurious quest. Therefore, he must be hungry. So perhaps I can entice him to accompany me to a nearby tavern.
Catherine:	Well, if the way to a man's head is through his stomach, I trust you will be successful, William!

[Shaking their heads, sadly, they make their way backstage.]

ACT I, Scene 3

The curtain partially opens upon Gilbert in his workshop, center stage. There is a table covered with suspicious looking chemical equipment. Dry ice bubbling away would be a nice touch. A heavy, ancient, and dusty tome rests on its own stand near the table.

Gilbert *[reading from the book]*: "…For gold stands as emperor, general, and judge of the mineral kingdom, and commands the lesser members of the kingdom. In the spirit of gold are to be discovered the warmth, mobility, flexibility, and tone of all the other metals. Therefore, the philosopher who would desire to discover the source of gold must seek said source in the proper conjoining of the metals and the elements: earth, air, fire, water..." Earth... yes, a beaker of pure earth from the sacred grounds of Canterbury. Fire... a coal from the hearth of the Archbishop himself. Water... indeed, a flask of the tears of the saints, direct from the Holy Lands. Air... what shall I do about the air? Where shall I find a purity of air?

[A knock on the door is heard. Gilbert moves to Stage Right, just behind the partially closed curtain, to answer the door.]

William! *[Gilbert is obviously surprised to see his old friend.]* You have come here? But I thought you did not approve of my pursuits. Why have you come? I warn you, I am very busy!

William *[placatingly, as he wanders around the room sniffing loudly]*: Gilbert, you are my dearest and my oldest friend in the world! *[He sniffs once more, shrugs his shoulders, and continues.]* I cannot bear to be at odds with you. You have been so taken up with your quest, and I with my own work, that we have spent almost no time together these past months. I fear our friendship has suffered, and, dear Gilbert, your friendship is most precious to me! Do you recall how we were used to spend idle hours arguing philosophy and discovering mathematical truths? The lazy picnics outside the city walls, wandering through the market stalls with Celia and Catherine...Gilbert, how goes Celia these days?

Gilbert *[as if waking from a deep sleep]*: Celia? Why, she is well, of course!

William: So you have seen her recently?

Gilbert: Recently... uh... I am certain that I have! That is, when last I saw her, she was very well!

William *[after gazing meaningfully out at the audience]*: Of course she was! But Gilbert—what say you to mine own dilemma? How can we manage to be together more often? Surely your work affords you time to sleep and eat and rest upon occasion?

Gilbert: Why, certainly, of course, to be sure!

William: Yes. Tell me of your most recent repast! How did you break your fast this morning?

[Gilbert is puzzled, frowning, trying to remember.]

William: Surely you remember how you supped last evening?

[Gilbert remains silent and puzzled.]

William *[clearly concerned]*: Gilbert, mine own dearest friend, surely you understand that, if you cannot recall how you dined, then it is very possible that you did not dine at all? Gilbert! How can you think, how can you seek out your puzzle with energy and concentration, if you do not give care to the needs of your body? My friend, you must allow me to treat you, at the very least, to stew and bread!

Gilbert *[somewhat stunned]*: Perhaps you have a point, friend William. I suppose I can spare an hour from my endeavors.

William *[heartily]*: That's my boy! You'll see, you'll be much the better for it!

Gilbert *[hesitating]*: Uh—William, what do you know of air?

The curtain closes.

ACT II, Scene 1

Mother enters from stage right. She is trudging home, across the stage, carrying a heavy basket of laundry and talking to herself. Master Duplicitous, without his wizard's robe, creeps out behind her, hiding and attempting to hear what she is saying. Behind Duplicitous creeps the Watchman, attempting to hear their conversation.

Mother: Oh! Alack and alas! That I should be cursed with such a dunce of a daughter! She will not listen to me, she does not understand me, she does not believe me! Why, I have years of experience in the world! I know whereof I speak! She responds to me as if I were an ignorant fool! What, oh, what am I to do?!!?

Master Duplicitous *[after turning to the audience and signaling that he is delighted at her distress]*: Ah, Mistress, Mistress! Surely a lady of such obvious distinction should not be carrying a burden such as this? Please, allow me! *[He staggers beneath the load as he takes up her basket.]* Why, Madam! This is a heavy burden indeed! Have you no servant, no helpful husband, no strapping son or dutiful daughter to help you?

Mother: If you think I am a lady, Sir, you sadly mistake the situation! For, although I was born into a titled family, I married for love and left my title behind me long ago. I have neither husband nor son, and as for a daughter... snort... daughter she is, but dutiful she most definitely is not!

Master Duplicitous *[clearly struggling under his load]*: But, Madam! You leave me speechless! How could any daughter worthy of the name abandon her dear mother to struggle with such a burden? Surely you jest.

Mother: Indeed, I do not jest. My fool of a daughter has lost her head over a boy and she no longer cares to speak with me or to help me. All she cares about is that idiot who chooses to spend his time in the fruitless pursuits of alchemy. Whilst I, who have years of experience in the world, am deemed a nothing in her sight. Oh, what could her father—may he rest in peace—have been thinking when he betrothed her to that boy all those years ago?

Master Duplicitous: Indeed, what could he have been thinking? Alchemy! Of all things! I suppose he is one of these young fools who have set their eyes on uncovering the secret of the Philosopher's Stone?

Mother: Yes, yes, the idiot! Why he could not put his talents to something useful, I know not! Why, I would open my heart and my house to him if he would! He is the third son of a butcher, for Heaven's sake! If it were not for the support of my husband—may he rest in peace—and me, he could never have received an education. And my dear husband—may he rest in peace—looked at me as he lay dying and said, "My dear, I have no qualms about going on to the next world, as I know that our dear Celia and her Gilbert will take care of you when I am gone. When they are wed, Gilbert shall move into our home. We have cared well for our girl, in providing her with an educated husband, as dear a boy as any girl could desire, who will find a place in the law and provide for her and you as well." Imagine! Imagine what my husband—may he rest in peace—would say now!

Master Duplicitous: Indeed, just imagine! These young people, Madam, simply have no respect for their elders and the sacrifices they have made. Why, even to own one's own home is no mean feat, with money and property as scarce as it is!

Mother: You speak truth there, Master… Master… Oh, pardon my manners! Sir, I think I have bent your ear with my complaints, and I do not even know your name!

Master Duplicitous *[catching sight of the Watchman, who has been following him and trying to overhear their conversation]*: I take no offense, Madam, as I know none was intended! And now, as we seem to have reached your doorstep, allow me to return to you your basket. A pleasure to serve you, Madam, a real pleasure!

[He bows and backs away, leaving her at the part in the curtain. She gazes after him, puzzled, then shrugs her shoulders and enters the "door."]

Mother *[turning back to the audience, basket on her hip and finger in the air]*: I have it! Yes, I have a plan! If Celia will not change her actions and if Gilbert will not abandon his foolish pursuits, I shall have to find someone responsible to attend to Celia, should anything befall me. Therefore, I shall bequeath our little house to my sister in Sussex, who loves Celia and is very sensible besides. That should convince Celia of the seriousness of my concern. It might even shake Gilbert out of his alchemical daydreams! It is one thing to play around with philosophy when one has a guaranteed home and a modest income, and quite another when one must work for one's lodging and meals!

ACT II, Scene 2

The curtain opens upon the Duchess, sitting in state, reading from a large scroll.

Duchess: ...And our great-grandmother Mathilda was wed to Henry, son of Edmund, and she was the first cousin, twice removed, of Stephen, son of... Oh! Our eyes! We cannot make out the name!

[She thumps on the floor with her cane, and Catherine enters.]

Catherine *[rather breathlessly]*: Yes, Your Grace?

Duchess: Catherine, child, come here and see if you can make out this name. It blurs before these ancient eyes.

Catherine *[approaching her and gazing at the scroll]*: Indeed, Madam, it is not your eyes, but rather the ink itself that is at fault. It is blurred in this space, as if it had been touched by water or damp.

Duchess: Then we are greatly relieved! We depend upon our eyes for observing those who come before us and determining their truthfulness. We greatly fear, my dear, that if these eyes were to weaken, many a practiced liar would go undetected. Why, England herself would suffer if these eyes lost their probity! Yes, you greatly relieve us, child.

Catherine: I thank you, Your Grace. I—Your Grace, forgive me. I hate to intrude upon your studies, but there is a—a certain person waiting in the antechamber who rather insistently demands to be allowed into your presence.

Duchess: Hmmm... And is this person, as you say, a male of indeterminate age, of average height and weight—in fact, entirely nondescript?

Catherine: But, Your Grace! You have described him perfectly!

Duchess *[sighing]*: Child, your protectiveness of me is most endearing. But, in this case at least, it is unnecessary. This is the bumbling Watchman who is endeavoring to retrieve for us our ancestral chalice. You may allow him into our presence.

[Catherine steps to the side to admit the Watchman, who is dressed in yet another costume. His head is bowed to the floor as soon as he is visible.]

Watchman: Your Grace! So honored! Your bountiful beauty baffles the sun! Your condescension is of a quality incalculable! Your presence...

Duchess: No presents for you, Sir! Indeed, if you have naught to report to us, you shall taste the darker side of our generosity! What say you?

Watchman: Your Grace, just this very morning I, in my diligence, discovered a dastardly deed, a demonic design, in short, a delicate and delicious debacle!

Duchess *[to Catherine, who is slowly backing out of the room]*: Catherine, my dear, pray do not abandon us to this demented detective! "Demented detective..."Alas! Now we are speaking as he does! Catherine! To what does he refer? Canst thou make it out?

Catherine *[staring hard at the Watchman, as if at a foreign species]*: Madam, I believe he intends to inform you that he has news. Determining whether or not this news has any bearing on your ancestral chalice may require our forbearance.

Duchess *[threateningly]*: Speak straight, Watchman. We are seriously displeased with your dithering.

Watchman: Indeed, Your Grace, I have seen, with my own eyes, a charlatan, a fraud, an impostor, a swindler engaged in his nefarious schemes in this very city! At your very doorstep!

Duchess: No doubt, young man, there are swindlers aplenty within the gates of this city. Was this particular swindler carrying an ancient cup?

Watchman: Your Grace, I have reason to believe that this churlish charlatan is the very cheat who charmed away your chalice! I have observed him, lo these many years, and his costume changes as changes his charge. Physician, philosopher, philanthropist—all are part of his pleasure, his pursuit, his practice. Your Grace, he could easily have stolen your cup! Why, he can even make at alchemy if it serves his desires!

Duchess: Very well, very well. Follow his footsteps, comprehend his conversations, disclose his den. But above all, find our cup! Now, go!

The Watchman bows his head to the ground and backs his way out, while Catherine looks on in barely concealed amusement and the Duchess massages her aching head.

ACT II, Scene 3

Mother walks out from behind the curtain and, staying to the side of the stage, begins to fold laundry from her large basket. Celia enters from the other side of the stage and stops short when she sees her. Celia takes a deep breath, steadying herself, and walks with purpose toward her mother. Mother does not look up from her work.

Mother: Ah, my dear, I am so glad you are home at last. I had begun to worry about you. I should not wonder, in fact, if I were about to go into a fret! Come, help me with these clothes. It is so difficult for one person to fold them neatly.

[Celia joins Mother at the basket.]

Mother: There's my good girl! *[Pause.]* My dear, I have given thought to our last conversation. *[Celia looks up, hopeful.]* The fact of the matter is that I am getting no younger. In fact, more and more these days, I feel the weight of my years. And I have concerns, Child, more than you could ever know.

Celia *[clearly anxious]*: Why, Mother, whatever could you mean? Is there something you have not told me? Is there something I should know?

Mother: Oh, no, no, no, Child, there is nothing for you to worry over. I am simply aware that no one lives forever, and that on that score, I am the same as everyone else. I need to make certain that you are provided for against that fateful day! *[She clasps her hands over her heart.]*

Celia: But, Mother, I shall be fine! Gilbert will always care for me! You need not be concerned! We shall do very well together, indeed. You have always said so, as did Father—may he rest in peace—before you!

Mother: But this is exactly the difficulty, of course. Gilbert has much on his mind as of late, to be sure. And I very much fear, my dearest, that what he has on his mind is not how best to care for you! No, you were always, and are still, the light of my life and the center of my world. It is up to me to see that you are provided for.

Celia: You provide for me very well indeed, Mother! Why, ever since Father died, we have not spent one little minute in anxiety over our state.

Mother: Ah. You have not been anxious, my dear, because I have protected you. But what if something should happen to me? No, no. You are my responsibility, not Gilbert's. And to that end, I have devised a plan—a perfect plan!

Celia: Yes, Mother? Might I ask what plan you have devised?

Mother: Well, of course. You know, Celia, how your father—may he rest in peace—and I had planned to deed to you and Gilbert our little home here?

Celia: Y-y-yes, Mother?

Mother: Well, I have been thinking. And I have decided that, as Gilbert is so engaged with his studies, I should be wiser to deed the house to someone of a solid, business-like mind, who would ensure that the house would be held in trust for you, just like your father—may he rest in peace—and I always wanted. So, I have decided to deed the house to my sister Polly, who lives in Sussex. You remember your dear aunt, do you not?

Celia: I-I-I... yes, I remember Aunt Polly. But, Mother...

Mother: No, no, no—there is no need to thank me! You have always been wise beyond your years, dearest Celia! It is understandable that you should be overcome with gratitude at the moment, for I know you realize how perfect is my little plan for protecting your future! Yes, your wellbeing is more important to me than anything else, and I know sister Polly will feel the same! Now, I must get these clothes back into the house. My, my, it looks as if it might rain!

Mother picks up her basket and exits, leaving Celia standing, stunned. Celia, in great distress, turns to the audience.

Celia: Oh! This is beyond my wildest imaginings! What shall we do? Alas, my Gilbert! What is to become of us? *[She begins to pace back and forth.]*

Catherine walks across the stage, a basket over her arm, silently counting off items on her shopping list. Celia enters from the other direction, head down, obviously distressed and distracted. She collides with Catherine and bursts into tears.

Catherine: Celia! Oh, my dear! Whatever is the matter?

Celia *[sobbing]*: Oh, Catherine, if you only knew!

Catherine: Tell me, tell me! What has happened?

Celia: Oh, Catherine, it is just too awful! First, Mother told me she plans to break my betrothal to Gilbert. Catherine! We have been betrothed since birth! How could she? We love each other!

Catherine: But, Celia, why would she do such a thing? Surely it was only in the heat of the moment. Surely she will change her mind?

Celia: NOOOO! She said the only thing that will cause her to change her mind is if Gilbert gives up his pursuit of alchemy, and that he will never do. Oh, Catherine, he is certain that he is close to discovering *[She looks around furtively and continues in a stage whisper.]* ...the Philosopher's Stone!!

Celia watches Catherine for her reaction. Catherine is duly impressed.

Catherine: Uh, Celia, forgive me for asking, but do you know exactly what the Philosopher's Stone is?

Celia: No, not exactly, but Gilbert says that, when he discovers it, he will have enough gold to ease the pain of the whole world. Imagine!

Catherine: Well, I am sure that is a most noble quest.

Celia: Yes, indeed, my Gilbert is as noble as a prince! But Mother thinks he is a fool! *[She begins to wail once more.]*

Catherine: Oh, my dear, I know your Mother! She is not unreasonable! Give her but a little time and she will relent.

Celia: NOOOO! You do not know the half of it! Just this minute, she told me that, if I do not abandon Gilbert, she will cut me out of her will entirely, and leave our house to her sister in Sussex! Gilbert and I will be totally lost! Oh, woe is me!

Catherine: Oh, my poor girl! Come with me back to my quarters. I will ease your brow with lavender and rose water and brew chamomile for you to sip.

Celia *[resolved]*: No. I must go to Gilbert immediately. He will know just what to do!

Celia runs off, behind the curtain, stage right. Catherine stands looking after her, clearly worried. After a few moments, she shakes her head and continues on toward the "market."

ACT III, Scene 1

At the center curtain, outside Gilbert's lodging. Celia runs onto stage, looks to right and left, and knocks on Gilbert's "door." Gilbert parts the curtains. Seeing Celia, he is clearly shocked.

Gilbert: Celia! What are you doing here?

Celia: Oh, Gilbert! Something awful has happened! You must let me in!

Gilbert *[scandalized]*: Celia! Although we are betrothed, we are not yet wed! Have you taken leave of your senses, to suggest that we be alone, in my lodging, without a chaperone? *[Celia wails.]* Here, here! Come, my heart! Let us sit ourselves in the park. No one would object to our sitting together in plain view!

[Unnoticed by either of them, Duplicitous sneaks out from stage left and makes his way closer and closer to them. He is trying to overhear their conversation.]

Gilbert *[solicitously]*: Now, now, my love! Do not take on so! Pray tell me, what has overset your sweet temper?

Celia: Oh, Gilbert, it is all too awful! Mother is determined that we shall not wed! And moreover, just this morning she said that, if you do not cease your quest for the Philosopher's Stone and find a position in law that will support our marriage, she will write me out of her will entirely and leave the house to her sister in Sussex! Oh, Gilbert! What are we to do?

Gilbert *[disturbed]*: Why, this is a disturbing turn of events! What shall we do, indeed?

Duplicitous *[who has come closer and closer as they have been talking and now approaches them directly, clearing his throat]*: Pardon, pardon, my young friends, but I could not help but overhear your distressing conversation! Perhaps I may be of assistance?

Gilbert: Why, it is Master Duplicitous! Celia, this is the master alchemist of whom I have spoken. He has helped me so much in my pursuits! Master, may I present Mistress Celia Simple, my betrothed.

Duplicitous: Delighted, my dear, I am sure! But, why these tears? For one of such beauty, surely the world has naught but gentleness and joy to offer? Why so woebegone, my child?

Celia begins to sob again.

Gilbert: Ah, Master! I fear we are at wits' end. We have been betrothed since birth. But Celia's mother, not understanding the seriousness of my alchemical work, and disappointed that I have not pursued a more ordinary profession, has threatened to write Celia out of her will and deed her house to another unless our betrothal is annulled. I fear we are lost.

Duplicitous: Now, now, my young friend? While there is life, there is hope! Let me think... *[He thinks, while Gilbert comforts Celia.]* Gilbert, you sense yourself to be near discovery, do you not?

Gilbert: Yes. It is only the lack of funds that prevents a fulfillment of my endeavors, I am certain.

Duplicitous: And have you anything to sell, which would help you raise the funds?

Gilbert: No, alas, for I am only the third son of a butcher. And, in truth, all my success in life I owe to Celia's father—may he rest in peace.

Duplicitous: And Mistress Celia, do you support this endeavor of your young prince here?

Celia *[avidly]*: With all my heart!

Duplicitous: And have you any possessions you could sell to raise the funds he needs to complete his work?

Celia: Alas, no. Everything I have belongs to my mother.

Duplicitous: And yet, I just heard you speak of the deed to a house.

Celia: Yes, but the house will only be mine if I turn my back on Gilbert. Else, my Mother will give the deed to her sister in Sussex.

Duplicitous [*standing and rubbing his hands together*]: Then, my children, your worries are at an end! [*He exults, while they look at him in confusion.*] Mistress, do you approach your mother in all contriteness, and go with her to the court to end your betrothal. [*Celia, appalled, backs away, handkerchief at the ready.*] Now, now, child! Hold your tears and listen! This will be a mere subterfuge on your part! Of course you do not wish to end your engagement with this fine lad! And you shall not, in your heart! But, when you make this agreement with your mother, she will then prove her good faith by handing over to you the deed to your house. You will then sell the deed to me. I will give the requisite funds to dear Gilbert. Gilbert will make his discovery, and all shall truly be gentleness and joy!

Celia and Gilbert are thunderstruck. Then they both begin to chatter at once, in excitement at the plan's perfection.

Celia: Oh, my goodness! It is a wonderful plan! A perfect plan! My mother, joyful in her victory, is certain to acquiesce!

Gilbert: Yes, and she will give you the deed, and the Master shall purchase it, and my work shall continue!

Celia [*wheedling*]: And, Gilbert darling, since you will make your discovery in such short order, it will not be so bad if we use just the tiniest portion of your gold to repurchase the house for Mother, will it?

Gilbert: Of course not, my love! After all, once we have the true Philosopher's Stone, we shall have access to all the gold we shall ever need!

Duplicitous: And, my children, to signify the good faith in which I enter into this arrangement, take this chalice. It is old, to be sure, and not worth much in itself. As it is made of base metal, perhaps it will be of use to you, Gilbert, in your experiments.

Gilbert *[taking the chalice, which is dull and stained]*: Thank you, Master! I shall indeed put it to good use! And if I am able to raise gold from its surface, you shall be the first—aside from my Celia, of course—to hear of it!

Duplicitous kisses the hand of Celia and claps Gilbert about the shoulders. The three part amicably.

Duplicitous *[pausing at the edge of the stage and speaking to the audience]*: There! In ridding myself of that infernal cup, I have killed two birds with one stone. Gilbert trusts me, and I no longer have to fret over the attentions of that interfering—and all too clever—Watchman. Ha! *[Exit.]*

PANTOMIME: A Tragical Interlude

Catherine enters and walks across the front of the auditorium and back again, carrying a sign that reads: "A Tragical Interlude." The Watchman and the Duchess take their places, backs to the audience, on the auditorium floor at stage right. Gilbert and William mirror them at stage left. Mother, Celia, and Duplicitous act out the following scene in "silent film" fashion: with short, choppy motions and pretending to speak very quickly. As they each "speak," a placard is held up in the air by one of the four cast members who are down on the auditorium floor. The placards indicate the gist of each character's words.

Mother pantomimes hanging up clothes from her basket. As Celia enters, Duplicitous sticks his head out from behind the curtain, trying to overhear their words.

Celia *[entering from stage right and crossing to Mother]*: Oh, dear Mother, I have had a change of heart!

Mother: Yes? A change of heart?

Celia: I have realized that you are right. I have put Gilbert behind me!

Mother: I know this was a difficult decision for you, but I am certain that you will not regret it!

Celia: And now, Mother, you'll be able to deed the house to me!

Mother: Oh, no, dear, you are far too young.

Celia: Mother, please may I have the house? I am not too young.

Mother: No, dear, Aunt Polly is much the better choice.

Celia walks away as Mother takes her laundry inside. Celia paces back and forth in despair.

Duplicitous *[magnanimous in his belief that Celia now has the deed]*: Give me the deed, my dear, and your worries will be at an end.

Celia *[increasingly frantic]*: But I do not have the deed!

Duplicitous *[incredulous]*: What?

Celia: Mother refused me, and I do not have the deed!

Duplicitous: What?!!? *[He pauses to think for a moment, then grabs Celia and, as she struggles, makes his way off stage with her.]*

ACT III: Scene 2

The curtain opens on Gilbert, pacing back and forth in his workshop. Periodically, he pauses, presses his hands to his head, and moans. The room is in even greater disarray than previously. The chalice given him by Duplicitous is clearly visible on his worktable, as are several flasks of chemicals. A knock sounds at the door. Gilbert ignores it. William cautiously peeks into the room. As he enters the room, the Watchman can be seen lurking in the background, in yet another disguise.

William: Gilbert? Gilbert? Whatever is the matter?

Gilbert: Matter, you say? Matter? Why, I do believe that matter itself is the matter! Yes! It is matter that has consumed all my resources, even my very flesh, and now shall no doubt destroy my heart! Matter! Oh, how I wish I had never heard the word! Alas! Alas!

William [*scratching his head and looking to the audience for help*]: Gilbert! Stop that pacing! You make no sense, Man! Calm down, be rational. Of what do you speak? [*He takes Gilbert by the shoulders and shakes him gently.*]

Gilbert: Oh, William! You cannot even imagine. Do you not understand? If I had not been so obsessed in transforming matter into gold, none of this would have happened. First, I spent all my funds. Second, I lost myself so entirely that I even forgot to eat or sleep. Third, I lost the good will of my dear Celia's mother. And now, I fear that I have lost my Celia as well! Oh, woe! Oh, woe!

William: Gilbert. [*He sighs deeply.*] Gilbert. You know I am your best friend. But, I swear to you, even a best friend has limited patience. And mine is nearly at an end. Now tell me, where is Celia, and why do you fear you have lost her?

Gilbert: Oh, William. I am so ashamed. I have been such a fool.

William: Yes, Gilbert, no doubt. But dwelling on the issue will not retrieve your Celia. I suggest you begin—at the beginning. [*Gilbert looks up.*] There's a good lad.

Gilbert [*sighing deeply*]: You know—well, I think that you do not know—that I am woefully short on funds for my research. In fact, I have only enough money to support me through perhaps another month, and then it is over. Finished. [*Sadly shakes his head.*] And Celia's mother said that, unless I were to give up this work and return to the law, she would give the deed to her house to her sister in Sussex, and Celia would have nothing. Well, Master Duplicitous [*William is incredulous. The Watchman, who has appeared to be nodding off, sits bolt upright and listens in perfect attention.*] suggested that Celia pretend to have thrown me over, and then her mother, in her joy, would give Celia the deed to the house.

William *[amazed, dumbfounded, outraged]*: Did you say "Master Duplicitous"?

Gilbert *[continuing on as before, unaware of William's distress]*: Yes, that is correct. And Master Duplicitous would then purchase the deed, and we would then have funds so that I could continue my work.

William: Gilbert, you idiot! Do you, with all your learning, not recognize that the very word, "duplicitous," means "dishonest, deceitful, and treacherous?" Gilbert! I hesitate to trust mine own ears! And then, when he has purchased the deed to the house, where would you have your Celia and her mother live?

Gilbert is struck speechless. The two friends stare at one another for a long moment.

William: Oh, never mind! What has come to pass? Why are you in such a state? Where is Celia?

Gilbert: Alas, I do not know! For I have this past hour received a communication from Master Duplicitous stating that Celia's mother refused to give her the deed. He states that he will have that deed, and that, if he cannot purchase it, he will exchange Celia for it. He has her in his keeping at this very moment! And, moreover, if the deed is not delivered into his hands by midnight, he will sell Celia into the hands of a corrupt sea captain who will make his profit by selling her as a servant in Virginia!

William: But... but... but, this is ghastly! Virginia is no place for a young girl, alone and without family or friends! I have heard that it is an awful place, a place of terrible storms, of lightning, hail, and even—it is reputed—snow!

Gilbert *[grasping his head in both hands]*: Alas, William, must you be so specific? My heart is breaking! This is all my fault! I cannot bear it!

Gilbert stumbles against his worktable, "spilling" the substance from one of his flasks onto the chalice that was given him by Duplicitous. Gilbert and

William both scramble to grab the various flasks before they break. William picks up the chalice.

William: But, Gilbert, what is this?

Gilbert: Oh, that. Master Duplicitous *[here, Gilbert almost breaks into tears]* gave it to me as a sign of his good faith. It is a nothing, a mere bauble of base metal for me to use in my experiments.

William: But, Gilbert, I think it more than a mere bauble. Look, you, here. Do you see how the dull surface has fallen away and reveals a shininess beneath?

The Watchman jumps to his feet. Knocking over any furniture in his way, and making a great deal of noise, he heads directly for the chalice.

Watchman: Hold! Hold, I say!

William and Gilbert look at one another, confused.

William: Hold what, my good man? And who are you?

Gilbert: And how came you to be inside my lodgings?

Watchman: I am a noble watchman, employed by the City of London and, of late, by Her Grace, the Duchess of Dishawash, to recover Her Grace's ancestral chalice. And, if I do not mistake me, young masters, this here cup is the very model of the very cup I seek! So hand it over, be good lads now.

William *[obviously thinking fast]*: No! No, you shall not have it!

Gilbert: William, what are you saying? Are you out of your mind?

William: I have never been saner, friend Gilbert. If this dutiful watchman wishes the return of Her Grace's cup, he will have to help us in a "returns" project of our own. Gilbert! Have you rope in your cupboard? Fetch it!

Gilbert obediently, if stunned, goes to the cupboard, not daring to turn his back on William. The Watchman splutters.

Watchman: Here now! What mean you? Her Grace means to have her chalice back, and I will take it to her! What dastardly deeds are you designing?

Gilbert, continuing to look at the Watchman, has his hand out to open the cupboard. Just then, the cupboard door opens a crack and a female arm reaches out, placing the rope in Gilbert's hand. The cupboard door closes and Gilbert holds the rope in both hands. Gilbert continues to stare at the other two men for a moment. Then he transfers his gaze to the rope in his hands. A look of horror gradually steals over his face.

Gilbert: W-W-W-William *[almost a whisper, then louder]*. William!

William *[irritated]*: What is it, Gilbert? Ah, good, you have the rope. Now, tie this watchman's arms to his sides.

Gilbert *[practically yelling]*: William! There is something very strange happening here!

William: Gilbert, what are you going on about?

Gilbert: William, unless I mistake me, this cupboard has acquired human characteristics!

Watchman and William: What?

Gilbert: I never opened the cupboard door! It knew what I wanted and it reached out and gave me the rope! It is not natural!

Watchman: Not natural! *[turning toward the door with an exaggerated tip-toe]* Well, young gentlemen, I'll just be on my way. Ancient ancestral ornaments is one thing. "Not natural" is another, and it's not for me!

William: Oh, no, you don't! *[grabbing his arm and turning him around toward the cupboard]* We'll solve this mystery soon enough!

William marches, in his best "Dudley Do-Right" fashion, toward the cupboard, holding the Watchman by his elbow. The three men gaze at the cupboard for a moment. Then William wrenches the door open. Catherine falls out into his arms.

All three men: Catherine!

They all gaze at one another in shock.

Catherine: But, William, Celia told me of the plan to sell the deed. So I came here and hid myself, thinking to stop the transaction in whatever manner I could contrive!

Watchman: What deed? Who is Celia?

William: This is where you come in, Sir! The self-same charlatan who gave my friend Gilbert this cup planned also to trick Celia and her mother out of their property. However, when his plan failed, he kidnapped Celia and is now holding her for ransom. And, if he does not receive that deed by midnight, he purposes to sell her into servanthood in Virginia! *[All gasp.]*

The door flies open and Mother appears, frantic and furious, pointing her finger at Gilbert.

Mother: I know you have her, you foul fiend! Where is she? What have you done with her?

Gilbert: I? I? Mother Simple, you much mistake the case! I know not where Celia is. Indeed, I myself am worried to distraction!

Mother looks around at the other faces.

Catherine: It is true, Mother Simple. None of us knows where Celia is.

After a moment's hesitation, as they all look at one another, Mother begins to wail. A disturbance is heard outside the door, as of things and people falling and being shoved.

Duchess *[peremptorily, from outside the door]*: Out of our way! Out of our way! *[She strides into the room, prepared for battle.]* Madam, you will cease that caterwauling! Watchman! Step forward, if you please!

Watchman *[bowing, head to ground]*: Y-y-y-yes, Your Grace. Of a certainty, Your Grace. Of your magnanimity, You Grace! With all due haste, Your Grace…

Duchess: Stop! This! Instant! Stand upright and explain this—this—this situation to us immediately!

Catherine *[pushing her way to the front of the crowd]*: I beg pardon, Your Grace, but, if it please Your Grace, may I explain?

Duchess: By all means! At least we would be assured of listening to a person of some sense. *[gazing witheringly at the Watchman, who shrinks away]*

Catherine *[beginning with great gusto and enthusiasm]*: Well, Madam, it all began when Gilbert... *[Gilbert and William, by now behind the Duchess and Mother Simple, implore Catherine through sign language not to reveal Gilbert's lack of judgment and good sense]* ...That is, perhaps it would be simpler if I began at what you see before you. *[Gilbert and William are visibly relieved.]* This chalice was given to Gilbert by Master Duplicitous, who is a wicked charlatan masquerading as an alchemist. He has—forgive me, Mother Simple, for speaking of that which you have not known until now—he has kidnapped our Celia and is demanding, in return for her safe return to us, that he be given the deed to Mother Simple's home. He demands that the exchange take place at midnight tonight, else he will sell our Celia into servanthood in Virginia! *[Everyone, including the Duchess, gasps, in unison.]*

Duchess *[reacting immediately as Mother begins to swoon]*: Here, quickly, take our smelling salts and wave them under her nostrils! *[Gilbert responds. Mother looks at him gratefully.]*

William: So you see, Madam, why I could not hand over the chalice!

Duchess: Why, of course, it is transparent!

The Watchman is clearly confused. Mother sees his confusion and jumps in.

Mother: Of course! We shall put it about that Gilbert's research has come to fruition, and that this chalice is the proof of it. For, see, here on the side, the dull finish has been torn away and it shines golden underneath. Then, when Duplicitous arrives for the deed, he will search the workshop for the cup, and we will seize him and throw him into the dungeon!

[Mother cackles and bounces in glee. All stare at her, open-mouthed at her cold-blooded audacity. The curtain closes.]

ACT III, Scene 3

Duplicitous creeps in from Stage Right, dragging a blindfolded, bound Celia with him.

Duplicitous: Now, my dear, just follow my directions and, unless I miss my guess, you will be freed in short order. But—you must do exactly as I say, do you understand?

Celia, who cannot speak because she has been gagged, nods her head.

Duplicitous: You are to stay right here where I place you, do you understand? You are neither to move nor to make a sound. If you do, it will not go well with you, and that I can promise! *[laughing wickedly]* Upon my honor!

He places Celia at the edge of the stage next to the curtain. He then walks, in an exaggerated tip-toe, over to the center of the curtain. He lifts his hand to knock, but the curtain mysteriously opens. All is silent in the workshop. Gilbert sleeps on the cot to the side. The worktable is neatly organized.

Duplicitous: Now, this is strange! It would seem that the door had not been latched. *[He spots Gilbert sleeping.]* Ah! My young friend must have left the door undone in expectation of my appearance. He tried to stay awake, but failed. What a pity! *[He makes his way over to Gilbert, who lies sleeping. He leans over the bed, searching with his eyes and hands for the chalice.]* Now, if I can manipulate events like a true alchemist, I shall have that chalice, Gilbert's secret formula for the Philosopher's Stone, and a tidy profit from the sale of the girl. Ha, ha, ha! I am too clever by half!

William, who is hiding under the bed, reaches out and grabs the feet of Duplicitous at the same time that Mother and the Watchman, who have been hiding under the worktable and then following him as he crosses over to the bed, grab his arms and attempt to tie his hands behind his back. Gilbert jumps up to assist them as Catherine, who has been hiding behind the bed, rushes out of the room calling for Celia. The cupboard door swings all the way open to reveal the Duchess, who waves her cane in the air and crashes it down upon the head of the still struggling Duplicitous. He struggles no more.

Duchess [*triumphantly*]: Here, here! Upon our dignity, we have not enjoyed ourselves so much in years! Watchman! There is a semi-bounteous berth in my dank and dirty dungeon that is keen to keep this charlatan for an uncounted and uncouth number of years. See that he is received there, posthaste!

Watchman [*bowing, head to the floor*]: Immediately, Your Grace! With perfect pleasure, I do declare!

Gilbert: Your Grace, may I present you with your ancestral chalice? I have taken the liberty to clean the rest of it for you, so now it appears in all its traditional splendor. It seems that, although I am an imperfect alchemist, I may yet earn my keep by peddling polish!

Duchess [*graciously accepting the chalice and admiring his work*]: Indeed, young man. [*Pause.*] Young man! It occurs to us that peddling polish would be an unfortunate use of time for one so talented. We have need of someone well-versed in the law to assist us in tending to public cases. Do you know anyone who might be interested in such a position?

Gilbert [*looking around and meeting Mother's eye and then grinning*]: In truth, I think I know just the person, Your Grace. In fact, if my soon-to-be mother-in-law here will agree, I myself will endeavor to assist you. That is, if it pleases you, Your Grace.

Mother: Gilbert, I can think of no better way to assure me that you will be a good match for my dear daughter, than for you to accept employment from Her Grace, our most munificent Duchess. My boy, you do possess the gift of being able to make and keep good friends. I have never seen anyone so blessed in this regard.

Celia [*suddenly strong*]: Yet, however blessed you might be, Gilbert, I cannot say that you always show good sense in the pursuits you choose to follow. Therefore, I beg you to consider me your foremost partner and consultant in these matters.

Mother [*shocked*]: Why, Celia, you have been transformed! You almost sound like a businesswoman!

Celia: Well, Mother, I have been thinking. And I have come to the conclusion that, if Gilbert and I are to make a life together, one of us needs to be practical. After all, we can't have Aunt Polly running our household!

Gilbert *[taking Celia's two hands in his own]*: Mother Simple, my beloved Celia, my dear friends: I think I owe it to you all to promise that, henceforth, I shall do my utmost to be at least a little practical, and to be a good husband for Celia. Moreover, I think I have learned my lesson. I shall endeavor to seek the warmth and light of gold where it does most good—not in the depths of the Earth, nor in the supposed secrets of the elements, but in the hearts of humankind.

The End

The Silver Shoes

Characters: Dorothy   Woman
                  Good Witch of the North   Man/Wizard
                  3 Munchkins   Guardian of the Gates
                  Scarecrow   Soldier
                  Tin Man   Wicked Witch of the West
                  Lion   Glinda, Good Witch of the South

The audience is arranged in a semi-circle in front of the stage, with clear aisles in the center and to left and right.

The Munchkins are hidden at first. Each wears blue clothing and a blue scarf or hat.

The teacher introduces play. Reminder that this will be different from the film, and that there are fourteen Oz books.

"And who can tell me what amazing and terrifying event sends Dorothy into Oz?... Yes! A tornado! Now, you know, we can't have a tornado inside our school. But we can imagine a tornado! Everyone, put your hands up in the air—way up high, and swirl them around and around. Be careful not to hit your neighbors! Now, can you make a scary wind noise? That's it! Louder and louder and..."

ACT I, Scene 1

[Dorothy, with Toto in hand, swirls onto the stage from SR and falls down in a faint. Wind noises stop. Silence. The Munchkins tiptoe in from around the outside of the hall, coming closer and closer to Dorothy and very curious about her.

From SL, 3 small people and 1 normal-sized person, female, enter, and gaze at Dorothy. After a moment, the female tiptoes closer for a look. Dorothy sits up, holding her head and the female steps back.]

Dorothy *[moaning]*: Oh, my head! Toto, are you all right? What happened? Where are we?

Female: Well, my dear, I cannot respond to your first two questions, but I can respond to the third. You are now in the Land of Oz. Welcome, most noble Sorceress, to the land of the Munchkins. We are so grateful to you for having killed the Wicked Witch of the East, and for setting our people free from bondage.

Dorothy: You are very kind, but there must be some mistake. I have not killed anything.

Female: Well, your house did, anyway, and that is the same thing. See! There are her two toes, still sticking out from under a block of wood.

[Dorothy looks and gives a cry of fright at the two feet, in silver shoes, poking out from under the set.]

Dorothy: Oh, dear! Oh, dear! The house must indeed have fallen on her! Whatever shall we do?

Female: There is nothing to be done.

Dorothy: But who was she?

Female: She was the Wicked Witch of the East, who has held the little Munchkins in bondage for, lo, these many years, making them slave for her both day and night. But now she is dead, and they are free, and they shall be forever grateful to you.

Dorothy: But who are the Munchkins?

Female: They are the people who live in this land of the East, where the Wicked Witch ruled.

Dorothy: Are you a Munchkin?

Female: No, but I am their friend, although I live in the land of the North. When they saw the Witch of the East was dead, the Munchkins sent a swift messenger to me, and I came at once. I am the Witch of the North.

Dorothy: Oh, my goodness! Are you a real witch?

Witch: But of course. But I am a good witch, and the people love me. I am not as powerful as the Witch of the East who ruled here, or I should have set the Munchkins free myself.

Dorothy: But I thought all witches were wicked.

Witch: Oh, no, that is a great mistake! *[laughing]* There were only four witches in all the Land of Oz, and two of them—those who live in the North and in the South—are good witches. I know this is true, for I am one of them myself, and thus cannot be mistaken. Those who dwelt in the East and the West were indeed wicked. But now that you have killed one of them, there is but one Wicked witch in all the Land of Oz. She is the one who lives in the West.

Dorothy: But Aunt Em has told me that the witches are all dead and died years and years ago.

Witch: Who is Aunt Em?

Dorothy: She is my aunt who lives in Kansas, where I come from.

Witch: I do not know where Kansas is, for I have never heard that country mentioned before. But tell me, is it a civilized country?

Dorothy: Oh, yes!

Witch: Well then, that accounts for it. In the civilized countries, I believe there are no witches left, nor wizards, nor sorceresses, nor magicians. But you see, the Land of Oz has never been civilized, for we are cut off from all the rest of the world. Therefore we still have witches and wizards amongst us.

Dorothy: Who are the wizards?

Witch: Oz himself is the Great Wizard. He is more powerful than all the witches together. He lives in the City of Emeralds.

[One of the Munchkins, who have all been standing by, silently polite, gives a loud shout and points to the spot where the Witch's feet were recently seen. The Witch looks and begins to laugh.]

Witch: Oh, my! She was so old that she dried up quickly in the sun! That is the end of her! But here, the silver shoes are yours, and you shall have them to wear. *[She reaches down, picks up the shoes, and hands them to Dorothy.]*

Munchkins: The Witch of the East was proud of those silver shoes, and there is some charm connected with them. But what it is, we never knew.

Dorothy *[taking the shoes]*: I am anxious to get back to my aunt and uncle, for I am sure they are worried about me. Can you help me find my way back?

[Witch and Munchkins look at one another and then at Dorothy, shaking their heads in unison.]

Munchkins: In the East there is a great desert, and none could live to cross it. In the South, there is a great desert, and none could live to cross it. In the West, there is a great desert, and none could live to cross it.

Witch: Moreover, in the West is the Wicked Witch of the West. And she would capture you and make you her slave. I live in the North, and...

Munchkins: ... In the North there is a great desert, and none could live to cross it.

Witch *[nodding head]*: Yes, I am afraid, my dear, that you will have to live with us.

[Dorothy begins to cry. The Witch takes out an "Eight Ball," shakes it up, and looks into the little window.]

Witch *[solemnly reading]*: "Let Dorothy Go to the City of Emeralds." *[She looks seriously at Dorothy.]* Is your name Dorothy, child?

Dorothy *[wiping her tears]*: Yes.

Witch: Then you must go to the City of Emeralds. Indeed, perhaps Oz will be able to help you in your quest.

Dorothy: Where is this city?

Witch: It is exactly in the center of the country, and it is ruled by Oz, the Great Wizard I told you of.

Dorothy: Is he a good man?

Witch: I can say that he is a good Wizard. Whether or not he is a man, I cannot tell you, for I have never seen him.

Dorothy: How can I get there?

Witch: You must walk. It is a long journey, through a country that is sometimes pleasant and sometimes dark and terrible. However, I will use all the magic arts I know of to keep you safe from harm.

Dorothy: Won't you please go with me?

Witch: No, I cannot do that, for I have responsibilities of my own, and the Magic Ball did not instruct me to attend you in the City of Emeralds. But I will give you my kiss, and no one will dare to injure a person who has been kissed by the Witch of the North.

[The Witch kisses Dorothy on the forehead.]

Witch: The road to the City of Emeralds is paved with yellow bricks, so you cannot miss it. When you get to Oz, do not be afraid of him, but tell your story and ask him to help you. Good-bye, child, and do not allow fear to get in your way.

[The three Munchkins bow low and exit, SL. The Witch nods at Dorothy, twirls about, and exits SL.]

ACT I, Scene. 2

Dorothy *[after thinking deeply for a moment]*: Well, Toto, it sounds like you and I have a long journey ahead of us. I wonder if I am dressed well enough to visit a Wizard? *[She looks down at her shoes.]* No. I think these shoes will never last for a journey, and I think they are too scruffy for a visit to a Wizard. I wonder if the Witch's shoes will fit me? What do you think, Toto? Surely, being a Witch's shoes, they would not wear out, no matter how far we must go. *[She takes off her shoes and tries on the silver ones.]* Oh, Toto! They fit perfectly! Now. We shall go to the City of Emeralds and ask the great Oz, the magnificent Wizard, to help us get back to Kansas.

[Dorothy sets off skipping down the center aisle. While the attention of the audience is on her, the Scarecrow slips out from SL and stands at the corner of the stage. He stands stiffly, as if he is suspended from a wooden cross-bar. Dorothy continues skipping until she obviously tires—about half way down the window aisle.]

Dorothy: Oh, my, I am tired! I have walked and skipped and skipped and walked until I feel quite overcome. Look, Toto, there is a nice farmer's field where we can rest. Why, it even has a scarecrow in it. *[She sits down on the edge of the stage & gazes at the Scarecrow. The Scarecrow does not move, but he does give her a slow and obvious wink. She jumps back, startled. She holds on to Toto, as if he were trying to jump out of her arms and attack the Scarecrow.]*

Toto! Stop! Behave yourself!

Scarecrow: Good day.

Dorothy *[startled]*: Did you just speak?

Scarecrow: Why certainly! How do you do, young lady?

Dorothy: I'm doing fairly well, thank you. How do you do?

Scarecrow: I'm not doing so well. It is very tedious being stuck here on a pole all day and all night, trying to scare away the crows.

Dorothy: Can't you get down?

Scarecrow: No, for this pole is stuck up my back. If you would take away the pole, I'd be very much obliged to you.

[Dorothy reaches up and "unfastens" the Scarecrow from the "pole."]

Scarecrow: Thank you so much. I feel like a new man. *[stretches, yawns, etc.]* By the way, who are you? And where did you come from? And where are you going?

Dorothy: My name is Dorothy, and this is Toto, and I'm from Kansas, and I'm going to the City of Emeralds to ask the wizard Oz to help me get back there again.

Scarecrow: Where is the City of Emeralds? And who is Oz?

Dorothy: You mean you don't know?

Scarecrow: No, in fact I don't know anything.

Dorothy: What do you mean?

Scarecrow: Well, in fact I don't have a brain, so it's quite impossible for me to know anything.

Dorothy: Really? But you look like you have a brain.

Scarecrow: Why, thank you, Miss Dorothy. I take that as quite a compliment. However, I assure you there's nothing between my painted-on ears except... straw. *[Sigh.]* Do you think Oz the wizard might give me some brains?

Dorothy: I really couldn't say, as I've never met the gentleman. However, if you like, you may come with me to see him. Even if he had no brains to give you, you wouldn't be any worse off than you are now.

Scarecrow: Very wise, very wise. And I will come with you. I don't mind that my legs and arms and body are stuffed, because that means I can't get hurt. If anyone were to stick a pin into me or step on my feet, I wouldn't mind because I wouldn't even feel it. But I do not want people to call me a fool, and if my head stays stuffed with straw instead of brains, how am I ever to know anything?

Dorothy: I am so sorry for you. Please, do come with me, and I'll ask Oz to do everything he can to help you.

Scarecrow: Thank you, Miss Dorothy. Will Toto mind if I accompany you?

Dorothy: Oh, don't worry about Toto. He never bites.

Scarecrow: I'm not worried about him. Remember—I can't be hurt, even if he does bite me. And I'll tell you something else, also. Not being made of flesh, I can't get tired. So I'll not be a burden to you on the journey. In fact, there is only one thing I am frightened of.

Dorothy: And, pray, what is that?

Scarecrow *[whispering]*: Please don't tell anyone. But my one fear is of a lighted match.

ACT I, Scene 3

[Dorothy and Scarecrow walk along the stage and down the steps on the other side. Scarecrow occasionally falls down with a flop but gets right up again, not at all bothered by falling.]

Dorothy: Doesn't it hurt you to fall down like that? Is there anything I can do to help?

Scarecrow: Oh, no! You see, as I am stuffed with straw, falling down does not hurt me at all! *[He starts to laugh, and she joins him.]*

Dorothy: Oh, my, I never thought of that! Of course you wouldn't be able to feel the bricks, if you're made of straw. Sometimes I wish I were made of straw! Wouldn't that be fun, Toto? *[She looks at Toto as she asks.]* Oh, goodness, I think all this walking and talking and laughing has made me hungry. Would you like something to eat?

Scarecrow *[laughing heartily]*: Oh, my! Miss Dorothy, I am never hungry! And to be truthful, it is a good thing I am not, for my mouth is only painted on, and if I cut a hole in it for eating, all the straw would come out of my head, and I should be a very strange looking fellow indeed!

Dorothy: Oh! Of course! So that means that I will not be rude if I eat in front of you without offering to share my food with you.

Scarecrow: Oh, no! Just eat away!

Dorothy: Thank you. I think I will. Let us sit here while I eat, shall we? *[They sit, and she takes a sandwich out of her basket and begins to eat.]*

Scarecrow: Well, now, as we are stopped for a while, tell me about yourself and the country you came from.

Dorothy: You would like to know about me? No one has ever asked about me before… hmmm. Well, as you know, my name is Dorothy. I am 12 years old, and in my country of Kansas, that is considered to be quite young. I live with my Aunt Emily and my Uncle Henry on a farm. We have a gray house—oh, I suppose it was painted a color at one time, but it is very windy and very hot and very dry where we live. There are not many trees, and I suppose the wind and the sun burned the paint off. So now our house is gray.

But I quite like it. We have one room with two windows and a door, and I sleep in a little bed in a corner nearest the stove. It is quite cozy, actually. Uncle Henry and Aunt Emily work very hard from sun-up to sun-down. My school is only two miles away, so I have not far to walk. I have only a few more months in school before I finish. Then I'll be able to help Uncle Henry and Aunt Emily on the farm, and surely three workers will mean that we can all work a little less so my aunt and uncle won't be so tired all the time.

Scarecrow *[silently considering what she has told him, and looking around at the scenery]*: Miss Dorothy, pardon my asking, but I cannot quite understand why you should wish to leave this beautiful country, where there are so many beautiful colors, and go back to the dry, gray place you call Kansas.

Dorothy: I suppose it is dry and gray. And when the wind blows, the dry, gray dust flies through the air and cuts my skin and lodges in my eyes. But I think you do not understand because you have no brains. If you did, you would understand that, no matter how dreary and gray our homes are, we people of flesh and blood would rather live there than in any other country, no matter how beautiful it is. After all, there is no place like home.

Scarecrow *[sighing]*: Of course I cannot understand it. If your head were stuffed with straw, like mine, you would probably live in a beautiful place, and then Kansas would have no people at all. It is fortunate for Kansas that you have brains.

Dorothy *[brushing off her hands after finishing her sandwich]*: No doubt you are right. Well, I am finished eating, and I feel quite refreshed. Shall we continue our journey?

Scarecrow: Yes, I think we should. *[peering down the center aisle]* I see that there is a tremendous forest ahead of us. Hmmm...the trees seem to be very close together. But, our road of yellow brick goes right into the midst of them. And if it goes in, no doubt it will come out on the other side. Wherever the other side may be.

Dorothy *[when they are half-way down the center aisle]*: No doubt you are correct. However, I must say I will be glad to be done with this forest. For I cannot see the sky beneath these branches, and I do like to see the sky. I suppose that is what comes of living in a place like Kansas.

Scarecrow: Why would Kansas have anything to do with it?

Dorothy: Well, you see, the sky in Kansas is so very big. Most of the time it is as blue as the blue of the Munchkins' land. But when there is a storm coming, you can see it far in the distance. And the clouds seem to fill the world. Those storms can be terrifying. That is how I got here, you know—there was a huge cyclone with a great cloud of gray dust, and it just picked up my house and brought Toto and me here.

Scarecrow: Without your Uncle and Aunt?

Dorothy: Yes, because they hid in our little cellar when the wind started and we saw the cyclone coming. But Toto started to run away, poor thing, and of course I couldn't let Toto be out in all that wind. So, instead of going down the ladder into the cellar, I reached out for Toto. And when I did, the cellar door slammed shut, and then the cyclone reached us, so Toto and I just hid under the bed. The house shook and rattled something awful!

Say, talking about all that dust and such makes me want to look for water.

Scarecrow: Why do you want water?

Dorothy: Well, to wash my face clean after the dust of the road, and to drink so the dry bread won't stick in my throat.

Scarecrow *[thoughtfully]*: It must be inconvenient to be made of flesh. It means that you must sleep, and eat, and drink. However, you do have brains. And it must be worth all the bother to be able to think properly. *[By now, they have walked down the center aisle, turned left, and come almost back to the front of the social hall.]* Look! I do believe there is a small stream there, falling down from a little spring.

[He points to the steps, SR.]

Dorothy: I do believe you are correct! *[She approaches the front of the steps, mimes washing her hands and taking a drink of water.]*

ACT I, Scene 4

[As she finishes drinking, she hears a deep groan nearby.]

Dorothy *[fearfully and quietly]*: What was that?

Scarecrow: I have no idea. But let us investigate.

[Just as he finishes saying this, they hear another groan, louder than the first, coming from behind the door, SR. Dorothy rushes up the steps to the door, opens it, and looks in.]

Dorothy: Oh, my! It is a man! Entirely made of tin! *[to the Tin Man, still unseen]* Did you make that noise?

Tin Man *[slowly and in a croaking voice]*: Yes. I did. I have been groaning for more than a year, and no one has ever come to help me before.

Dorothy *[in much sympathy for the sadness in his voice]*: Can I do anything to help you?

Tin Man: If you will look just there, you will see an oil can. I would be so much obliged if you would oil my joints. They are rusted so badly that I cannot move them at all, but if I am well oiled, I shall be able to move again.

Dorothy *[searching among the undergrowth]*: Ah! Is this an oil can?

Tin Man: To be sure!

Dorothy: But where are your joints?

Tin Man: Oil my neck first. *[She does, and he sighs with relief.]* Now I shall be able to speak without pain. Now oil my hands, and wrists, and elbows, and shoulders. *[She does, and he sighs even louder.]* Oh, I cannot tell you what a comfort this is! Now, if you please, oil my waist, and my hips, and my knees, and my ankles, and my feet! *[She does, and he sighs even LOUDER.]* Oh, thank you, thank you, thank you, kind, kind lady! *[He lurches onto the stage, thanking her again and again.]* Oh, my goodness! I might have stood there forever and turned completely into rust with the rain, if you had not come along! I was here because I am a woodman, and I chop wood. Why are you here?

Dorothy: We are on a journey to visit the City of Emeralds and to see the great and magnificent Oz, who I understand is a wise and powerful wizard.

Tin Man: Why do you wish to see Oz?

Dorothy: I want him to send me back to Kansas, and Scarecrow here wants the wizard to give him a few brains for his head.

Tin Man *[thinking deeply for a moment]*: Do you suppose the wizard Oz could give me a heart?

Dorothy: Well, I guess he could. Giving you a heart would be as easy as giving brains to Scarecrow.

Tin Man: True. If you will allow me to join your little party, I will also go to the City of Emeralds and ask Oz for his assistance.

Scarecrow *[with great enthusiasm]*: Well, come right along! Miss Dorothy and I have been having such a lovely time together. Your presence will only increase our pleasure!

Tin Man *[picking up his ax and placing his oil can in Dorothy's basket]*: Oh, thank you, my new friends! We shall have a jolly time together!

[They begin to walk toward the center aisle once again. Dorothy appears to be lost in thought, and she doesn't notice when Scarecrow stumbles and falls to the side.]

Scarecrow: Help! Oh, help! Miss Dorothy! Tin Man!

[They rush to help Scarecrow regain his footing.]

Tin Man: But why didn't you walk around that hole?

Scarecrow: I don't know enough to walk around a hole! *[cheerfully]* My head, you know, is stuffed with straw. And that is why I am on my way to visit Oz and to ask him for brains.

Tin Man: Oh! I see! But you know, brains are not the best things in the world.

Scarecrow: Have you any brains?

Tin Man: No, my head is quite empty. But once I had brains and also a heart. And I must say, having tried them both, I would much rather have a heart.

Scarecrow: But why is that?

Tin Man *[looking down the center aisle]*: As we have a ways to go, if you are interested, I will tell you my story as we walk.

I was born a child of flesh and blood just like Miss Dorothy here. When I grew up, I became a woodchopper just like my father before me had been. When he died, I took care of my old mother for as long as she lived. Then, when she died, I made up my mind that I did not wish to live alone. One of the Munchkin girls who lived nearby was so beautiful and kind that I decided to ask her to marry me, for I found that I loved her with all my heart.

She promised to marry me as soon as I had earned enough money to build her a better house. So I set to work harder than ever. But the girl lived with an old woman who did not wish her to marry anyone—this old woman was so lazy she wished the girl to stay with her and do all the cooking and housework. So, this old woman went to the Wicked Witch of the East and promised her two sheep and a cow if she would prevent the marriage.

The Witch therefore enchanted my ax. When I was chopping away one sunny day, the ax slipped and cut off my left leg. So, I went to a tinsmith and asked him to make me a new leg out of tin. This leg worked very well, once I had practiced using it. But this angered the Witch, because after all she had made a promise. So one day my ax slipped again and cut off my right leg. And again the tinsmith came to my aid.

The Witch was VERY angry by this time. So, one after the other, my ax slipped and cut off my left arm, then my right arm, then my head. Each time the tinsmith replaced the part with tin, and I learned how to work with it, and my girl and I continued to plan to marry. But finally, in the Witch's great anger, she caused my ax to slip and cut my body right in two. My friend the tinsmith created a new one for me, of course. But alas! I had no heart! And I no longer cared whether I married my Munchkin girl or not.

I was, however, very proud of my shiny body, so I didn't mind very much that I was not married. But one day, as I was out in those woods back there chopping away, a great rainstorm came up. By the time the rain had stopped, my joints had rusted stiff, and my oil can was out of my reach.

Now I know that when I was in love, I was the happiest man alive. So I wish to ask the great Oz for a heart so that I can go back to my girl and ask her to marry me once again, and take her away from that old woman.

Scarecrow *[thoughtfully]*: Yes, I can see full well why you would wish for a heart. But I shall ask for brains instead, for if a man is a fool, he won't know what to do with a heart if he has one.

Tin Man: And I shall ask for a heart, for brains do not make one happy, and happiness is the best thing in the world.

Dorothy: And I shall think on this. I wonder which of you has it the right way. Which is more important? A brain, or a heart? Well, I guess if I can only get back to Kansas, I won't need to wonder about that any more.

[By this time, they have walked down the center aisle, turned right, and again find themselves in front of the stage.]

ACT I, Scene 5

Dorothy *[shivering]*: Oh, dear. This forest seems to go on forever. And I keep hearing growls and roars from far away. How much longer, do you think, before we are out of it altogether?

[Just as she finishes speaking, there is a low growl from offstage.]

Tin Man: That I cannot tell you, for I have never been all the way through this forest, nor have I ever been to the City of Emeralds. *[reminiscing]* My father went there once, when I was a boy, and he said it was a long journey through a dangerous country. But he also said that the country near the City is once again a beautiful country, no doubt from the influence of the great Oz. But never fear, Miss Dorothy! As long as I have my oil can, I fear nothing! And nothing can hurt the Scarecrow, and the Good Witch has kissed you, so you are entirely protected from harm on all sides.

Dorothy *[a little frantically]*: But there's Toto! What will protect Toto?

Tin Man: Why, we must protect him ourselves, if need be.

[Just as he finishes, there is a terrible roar from off stage. Almost immediately a Lion bounds onto the stage. Dorothy screams, the Scarecrow and the Tin Man jump back, startled, and Toto appears to try to jump out of Dorothy's arms. Dorothy wrestles with the little fellow, crying out, "Stop! Stop! Toto, no!" etc. The Lion strikes out at the Scarecrow, sending him tumbling to the side. Then he strikes at the Tin Man, who also falls to the ground. Dorothy, fearing that Toto will be next, dashes up and slaps the Lion on the nose and cries out.]

Dorothy: Don't you dare strike my friends! You should be ashamed of yourself, hitting two innocent and peaceful fellows like that and threatening my little Toto! Don't you dare bite him!

Lion *[whimpering and rubbing his nose where Dorothy struck him]*: I didn't bite him.

Dorothy *[still angry, frightened, and yelling]*: No, but I could tell you were going to!

Lion *[still rubbing his nose and whimpering]*: I didn't bite him!

Dorothy: No, but you were going to! You are nothing but a big coward!

Lion *[starting to truly cry, and hanging his head in shame]*: Awww... why did you have to say that? It's the truth, I know it. I am a big coward. I've always been a big coward, so how can I help it?

Dorothy *[indignant]*: I don't know, I'm sure! To think of it, striking an innocent straw man!

Lion *[surprised]*: You mean he's stuffed?

[Dorothy picks up the Scarecrow and helps him find his footing again, patting him into shape & replacing some of the straw which has spilled out.]

Dorothy: Of course he's stuffed!

Lion: So that's why he went over so easily. I was astounded to see him twirl around so. Is the other one stuffed as well?

Dorothy: No, he's made of tin, and he never hurt another soul.
[Dorothy helps the Tin Man get to his feet, polishing him with her apron.]

Lion: So that's why he nearly blunted my claws! When they scratched against the tin, it made a cold shiver run down my back. And what is that little animal you are so protective of?

Dorothy *[holding Toto up to her chin]*: This is my dog, Toto.

Lion: And which is he—stuffed, or made of tin?

Dorothy: Why, neither, of course! He is made of—um—meat.

Lion: Well, he certainly is a curious little animal. He seems remarkably small, now that I see him up close. *[sadly]* No one would think of biting such a small creature except for a coward like me.

Dorothy: What makes you such a coward?

Lion: It's a true mystery. I suppose I was born that way, and it certainly is a burden for me. The lion is called the King of the Beasts and is supposed to have more courage than any other beast of the forest. But whenever I meet a tiger or a bear, or even a man, I just roar loudly and they run away. So I never have to do anything else. No one has ever challenged me before now. If they had, I would have run away myself, I am such a coward.

Scarecrow *[dusting himself off]*: But that isn't right! The King of the Beasts should not be a coward.

Lion *[wiping away his tears with the tip of his tail]*: I know. It is a great sorrow, and it makes my life very unhappy. But whenever I come close to danger, my heart beats very fast and very hard.

Tin Man *[taking out a little brush and cleaning himself]*: Perhaps you have a disease of the heart.

Lion: Perhaps I do.

Tin Man: If you do, you ought to be glad, you know, for it proves you have a heart. As for me, I have no heart. *[sigh]* So I cannot have a heart disease.

Lion *[thoughtfully]*: Perhaps if I had no heart, I should not be a coward.

Scarecrow: Do you have brains?

Lion: I suppose I do. I've never looked to see.

Scarecrow: I am on my way to the City of Emeralds, to see the Great Wizard, to ask him to give me some brains, for my head is stuffed with straw.

Tin Man: And I am going to see the great Oz, to ask him to give me a heart. For where my heart should be, there is only a great emptiness.

Dorothy: And I am going to see the great wizard, to petition him to help Toto and me get back to our home in Kansas. For you know, there is no place like home.

Lion [*shyly*]: Do you think the powerful Oz might give me some courage?

Scarecrow: I think that would be just as easy as giving me some brains.

Tin Man: Or giving me a heart.

Dorothy: Or sending us home to Kansas.

Lion: Then, if you don't mind, I will accompany you to the City of Emeralds, for my life is simply unbearable without having one single jot of courage.

Dorothy: You will be very welcome. For in spite of your lack of courage, your very presence will help keep away any other beasts. Although it seems to me that they must be even more cowardly than you are, if they allow you to scare them so easily.

Lion: They really are. But that doesn't make me any braver, and as long as I know myself to be a coward, I shall be unhappy.

[*They all walk across to SL together. As they approach the other side, the Tin Man suddenly shouts out.*]

Tin Man: Oh, no! I have stepped on a beetle and it is quite dead! [*He begins to cry, loudly at first, and then more quietly as his mouth rusts shut.*]

Dorothy: Why, whatever is the matter? *[The Tin Man gestures to Dorothy very broadly to take out his oil can, but she doesn't understand him. Nor does the Lion, though they are obviously very puzzled and trying different things that might help.]*

Scarecrow: Oh! I see what he needs! Miss Dorothy, will you kindly pass me that oil can? *[He then oils the Tin Man's mouth. The Tin Man works his mouth around and finally begins to speak.]*

Tin Man: Oh, thank you, my friend, you are so very clever! This will certainly serve me a lesson, to look where I step. For if I should kill another bug or beetle, I should surely cry again, and that will only rust my jaws again so that I will not be able to speak. You people of flesh and blood have something to guide you so that you need never do wrong. But I have no heart, so I must be very careful. After the wise Oz gives me a heart, I shall not need to be so careful.

ACT II

[After ACT I, a dark strip of cloth, about three feet wide, is placed across the floor in front of the audience. A balance beam is to one side on the stage.]

ACT II, Scene 1

The four friends enter from the back of the hall, making their way down the SL aisle and talking as they come.

Dorothy: I declare, sometimes I wonder if we will ever find our way out of this forest. Do any of you know how much further we will have to travel?

Scarecrow: If I had a brain, I dare say I would know. But as I have no brain, I don't.

Tin Man: I was rusted for so long that all around me changed, and I don't recognize this part of the forest at all.

Lion: Umm... ahem... umm...

Scarecrow: Well, speak up if you have something to say!

Lion: I—er—I believe we are approaching that part of the forest in which the Kalidahs live.

Tin Man: The Kalidahs? What a strange-sounding name!

Lion: Yes, and if my memory serves me correctly, they are a mighty strange-looking breed as well.

Dorothy *[spotting the "ditch" and clearly alarmed by it]*: Can you remember to tell us about them after we figure out how to get across this huge ditch? *[They all line up along the edge of the cloth.]*

Scarecrow: My, my, my. We certainly can't step across it.

Dorothy: And it's far too steep to climb down and then climb up again on the other side. Whatever shall we do?

Tin Man: I haven't the faintest idea.

Scarecrow: We cannot fly, that much is certain. Therefore, I suppose if we cannot cross it, we must just stop where we are.

Lion *[measuring the distance carefully with his tail]*: I think I could jump over it.

Scarecrow: Oh! Then we will be fine, for you can carry us over on your back, one at a time!

Lion: Well, I'll try it. Who'll go first?

Scarecrow: I'll go first, for if you found that you could not jump over the gap, Dorothy would be killed, or the Tin Woodman badly dented on the rocks below. But if I am on your back, it will not matter so much, for the fall would not hurt me at all.

Lion: I am terribly afraid of falling, myself, but I suppose there is nothing to do but try it. So, get on my back and we will jump away.

[The Scarecrow places his arms around the Lion's neck. The Lion walks to the edge and crouches down.]

Scarecrow: Why don't you run and jump?

Lion: Because. That isn't the way we lions do these things. *[And together they jump over the "gully." Then, as soon as the Scarecrow lets go of the Lion's neck, the Lion jumps back over the gully.]*

Dorothy: We'll go next, won't we, Toto? *[She places her arms around the Lion's neck, and they jump. The Lion turns right around, jumps, collects the Tin Man, and jumps back over the ditch. They all breathe deeply and continue on their way, up the stairs at SR.]*

Dorothy: Oh, Lion, thank you so much. That was quite brave of you, you know. Now, tell us about the K-K-K...

Scarecrow: Kalidahs.

Lion: They are monstrous beasts with bodies like bears and heads like tigers. And I'm terribly afraid of them.

Dorothy: I'm not surprised that you are. They must be dreadful beasts.

[They have walked toward the center of the stage and arrive at another gulf—a black cloth about six feet wide—across their path.]

Lion: Oh, dear. I know I can't jump across that.

Tin Man: Then what shall we do?

Scarecrow: Hmmm. *[He looks around.]* Look over there! I see a fallen tree that looks longer than the gulch is wide! *[He sees the balance beam.]* What if we lift it up and swing it over to the other side? Wouldn't that make a sort of bridge for us? And if we're very careful, we should all be able to cross over.

Lion: Oh, what an excellent idea! One would almost suspect you had brains in your head, instead of straw.

[Scarecrow and Tin Man lift the balance beam and swing it over the "gulch." They all gather at their end, preparing to cross. Suddenly, there is a frightful roar! (The audience has been encouraged to make this terrifying sound.)]

Lion: They are the Kalidahs! *[trembling]*

Scarecrow: Quick! Let us cross over!

[Dorothy, with Toto, goes first, followed by the Tin Man and the Scarecrow. The Lion, trembling, turns to face the Kalidahs. He gives a loud and terrible roar, frightening Dorothy, who screams, while the Scarecrow falls over backward off the "log" and onto the land. The Tin Man pulls Dorothy away from the "log" as the Lion bounds across it.]

Lion *[shouting]*: We are lost, for they will surely tear us to pieces with their sharp claws! But stand close behind me, for I will fight them to protect you for as long as I can stay alive!

Scarecrow: Wait a minute! Tin Man, help me out here. Quickly! Let us pull this log over to our side! *[They do.]* Now! Let the Kalidahs come on! We are safe on this side of the gulch.

Lion *[breathing a deep sigh of relief]*: Well, I see we are going to live a little while longer, and I am glad of it, for it must be a very uncomfortable thing not to be alive. Those creatures frightened me so badly that my heart is beating still!

Tin Man: Ah. Alas. I wish that I had a heart to beat.

Dorothy: We must journey on until we arrive at the City of Emeralds and make our petitions to the wizard, Oz. Then, my friends, you will have a heart. And you will have a brain. And you will have courage. And perhaps I will even be able to return to Kansas. I know my aunt and uncle are worried about me, and I miss them dreadfully. And Toto does, too. Don't you, Toto?

Tin Man: Of course, Miss Dorothy, you are right. And here are more yellow bricks, to help us find our way.

ACT II, Scene 2

[They all continue across to the steps at SL and go down the steps. As they come to the main floor, we see that there are people sweeping, stirring big pots, hoeing, washing clothes—all in pantomime. These people have green scarves or hats and other accessories.]

Scarecrow: I say, Miss Dorothy, I do believe we must be getting close to the City of Emeralds.

Dorothy: Why do you say that?

Scarecrow: Why, I've just noticed that the people we are passing on this road are all dressed in green. And the houses are green, also. Would it not seem that green would be the favorite color of people who live near the City of Emeralds?

Dorothy: Do you know, I do believe that you are correct! This must be the Land of Oz. Oh, surely we are getting close to the great wizard! And I am getting to be very hungry.

Tin Man: Perhaps we could stop at one of these green houses and ask the inhabitants for a little food for you.

Lion: I don't know. These people don't seem very friendly. And I am quite worried about talking to unfriendly people.

Tin Man: I think no one likes to talk with unfriendly people, Lion. However, Miss Dorothy is made of flesh like you yourself are, and she requires sustenance.

Lion: That is true. *[sighing]* If Miss Dorothy is hungry, I will overcome my fear.

[They stop at a "door" and knock. A woman in green—who is the same actress as the one who plays the Good Witch—answers the door and looks at them suspiciously.]

Woman: What do you want, child, and why is that great lion with you?

Dorothy: We are strangers in this land, but we are journeying from the Land of the Munchkins, and I am very hungry. My friends are not made of flesh and so do not feel hunger. But have you any food you could share with me? And the Lion is my friend also, and he would not hurt you for the world.

Woman: Is he tame? *[opening the door a little wider]*

Dorothy: Oh, yes. And he is a great coward, too, so he is more afraid of you than you are of him.

Woman: Well, if that is the case, you may sit under our tree and I will bring you food. But the lion must behave.

[The Woman closes the door for a moment and returns with her husband—who is the same actor who will later play the part of the Wizard—and a plate on which are bread, an apple, and cheese. Dorothy takes the plate with a pleasant "thank you"; and the four friends sit under the tree.]

Man: Where are you all going?

Dorothy: We are on our way to the City of Emeralds, to meet with the great wizard, Oz.

Man: Oh, indeed! Are you certain that Oz will meet with you?

Dorothy: Why would he not?

Man: It is said that he never lets anyone come into his presence. I have been to the Emerald City many times, and it is a beautiful and wonderful place. But I have never been permitted to see the Great Oz, nor do I know of any living person who has seen him.

Scarecrow: Does he never go out?

Man: Never. He sits day after day in the great throne room of his palace, and even those who wait upon him do not see him face to face.

Tin Man: What is he like?

Man: That is hard to tell. You see, Oz is a great wizard, and he can take on any form he wishes. So some say he looks like a bird, and some say he looks like an elephant.

Woman: And a neighbor once told me he looks like a cat!

Man: Yes! And to others he appears as a beautiful fairy, or a gnome, or any other form that pleases him.

Woman: But who the real Oz is, when he is in his own form, no living person can tell.

Dorothy: This is all very strange. However, we must try, in some way, to see him, or we shall have made our journey for nothing.

Man: Why do you wish to see the terrible Oz?

Scarecrow *[eagerly]*: I want to ask him to give me some brains!

Man: Oh, Oz could do that easily enough. He has many more brains than he could possibly need.

Tin Man: And I need to ask him if he could give me a heart.

Woman: That should not trouble him, for Oz has a large collection of hearts, of all sizes and shapes.

Lion: And I hope he will give me some courage.

Man: Oh, Oz keeps a great pot of courage in his throne room, which he has covered with a golden plate to keep it from running it over. He will be happy to give you some.

Dorothy: And I will ask him to send me back to Kansas.

Woman *[surprised and puzzled]*: Where is Kansas?

Dorothy: Alas, I do not know. But it is my home, and I'm sure it's somewhere.

Woman: Very likely. Well, Oz can do anything, so I suppose he will find Kansas for you. But first you must get to see him, and that will be a hard task. For the Great Wizard does not like to see anyone, and he usually gets his way. *[speaking to Toto]* But what do you want? *[Toto simply "arfs" a little in return.]*

[By this time, Dorothy has finished eating. The four friends thank the Woman and the Man and continue their walking down the aisle SL. They turn the corner at the back and start up the center aisle.]

ACT II, Scene 3

Dorothy *[seeing the backdrop of the Emerald City]*: Look! That must be the City of Emeralds itself!

[They skip along down the aisle. Dorothy picks up the chime at the base of the stage and strikes two notes. A man dressed all in green enters, walking like a soldier, from SR. He stops at center stage and looks at them.]

Guardian: What do you wish in the City of Emeralds?

Dorothy: We have come to see the Oz, the great and wonderful and terrible wizard.

Guardian *[quickly sitting down in shock]*: It has been many years since anyone asked me to see the Wizard. He is indeed wonderful and terrible, and powerful as well. And if you have come on an idle or foolish errand to bother the wise reflections of the Great Wizard, he might become angry and destroy you all in an instant!

Scarecrow: But it is not a foolish errand, nor is it an idle one. It is important. Moreover, we have been told that Oz is a good wizard.

Guardian: So he is. And he rules the Emerald City wisely and well. But to those who are not honest, or who approach him out of curiosity, he is most terrible. Few have ever dared to ask to see his face. I am the Guardian of the Gates, and since you demand to see the Great Oz, I must take you to his palace. But first you must put on these spectacles.

Dorothy: Why?

Guardian: Because if you did not wear spectacles, the brightness and glory of the Emerald City would blind you. Even those who live in the City must wear spectacles night and day. They are all fastened on, for Oz so ordered it when the City was first built. I have the only key that will unlock them.

[He opens the big box, which is filled with spectacles of every size and shape, all with green lenses. The Guard finds glasses for all four friends and "locks"

them into place. He then puts on his own glasses and directs them to enter the "portal"—the door at SR—into the city.]

[The four companions are dazzled by the people, all dressed in green, walking about. They look about them in wonderment. The Guard leads them from SR to the center of the stage, where they meet a Soldier, also dressed in green.]

Guardian: Here are strangers, and they demand to see the Great Oz.

Soldier: Please be seated, and I will carry your message to the Great and Terrible Wizard.

[Taking his leave, the Guardian salutes the four friends and exits, SR. They sit on the bench, obviously frightened. The Lion lies on the floor at their feet. Shortly, the Soldier returns.]

Dorothy: Have you seen the terrible Oz?

Soldier: Oh, no, I have never seen him. But I spoke to him as he sat behind his screen, and I gave him your message. He said he will grant you an audience, if you so desire. But each one of you must enter his presence alone.

Dorothy: Thank you so much, you are very kind. We were so worried that the wizard would refuse to see us.

Soldier: Oh, he will see you—although he does not like to have people ask to see him. Indeed, at first he was angry at your request and said that I should send you back to where you came from. But then he asked me what you looked like, and when I mentioned your silver shoes, he was very much interested. At last I told him about the mark upon your forehead, and he decided that, after all, I could admit you into his presence.

[Just then, a gong sounds.]

Soldier: That is the signal. Now you must go into the throne room.

[Dorothy disappears behind the partition. We hear her speak to the Wizard as well as his responses. The others freeze.]

Dorothy: If you please, Sir, I am Dorothy, the small and meek. I have come to ask you for help.

98

Wizard: Where did you get the silver shoes?

Dorothy: I got the silver shoes from the Wicked Witch of the East, when my house fell on her and killed her.

Wizard: Where did you get the mark on your forehead?

Dorothy: Oh, the mark on my forehead? That is where the good Witch of the North kissed me when she bade me farewell and sent me to you.

Wizard: What do you ask of me?

Dorothy: If you please, Sir, I would like for you to send me back to Kansas, where my Aunt Emily and my Uncle Henry are. Your country is indeed very beautiful, but it is not my home. It is strange to me, and I do not like it. And I am certain that my aunt and uncle must be dreadfully worried about me, I have been away for so long.

Wizard: Why should I do this for you?

Dorothy: You should do this for me, because you are strong and I am weak. Because you are a Great Wizard and I am only a helpless little girl.

Wizard: But you were strong enough to kill the Wicked Witch of the East.

Dorothy: But killing the Wicked Witch of the East just happened when my house fell on her. I could not help it.

Wizard: If I help you, I will do so on one condition: You must kill the Wicked Witch of the West.

Dorothy: What!??! You expect me to kill the Wicked Witch of the West? Sir! I understand that you want payment for helping me return to Kansas. But surely you know that killing the Witch is impossible! I told you, I didn't mean to kill the Wicked Witch of the East, and I have no idea how I could kill the Wicked Witch of the West! I know I wear the silver shoes, but they mean nothing to me but a way to walk without hurting my feet! And if you, who are great and powerful, cannot kill her yourself, how do you expect me to do it?

[Dorothy returns, weeping, to her friends.]

Dorothy *[with great sadness]*: There is no hope for me. For Oz will not send me home until I have killed the Wicked Witch of the West, and that I can never do.

[The gong sounds again.]

Soldier: Come, Scarecrow, for Oz now summons you.

[The Scarecrow disappears behind the partition in great fear and trembling. The others freeze.]

Scarecrow: Oh, Wise and All-Powerful Wizard, I am only a Scarecrow, stuffed with straw. Therefore I have no brains, and I come to you praying that you will put brains in my head instead of straw, so that I may become as much a man as any other in your dominions.

Wizard: Why should I do this for you?

Scarecrow: I think you should do this for me because you are wise and powerful, and because no one else can help me.

Wizard: If I do this for you, it will not be because no one else can help you. If I do this for you, I will do it because you have killed the Wicked Witch of the West.

Scarecrow: What? You want me to kill the Wicked Witch of the West? But I thought you told Dorothy you wanted her to do that.

Wizard: Nevertheless, I lay this charge upon you as well.

[The Scarecrow returns to his friends.]

Scarecrow *[sorrowfully]*: Indeed, Dorothy, it is the same for me. He demands that I kill the Witch, and as I do not know how I could do such a thing, all is lost, and I shall never have the brains I so desperately desire.

[After a moment or two, the gong sounds again.]

Soldier: Come, Tin Man, the great Oz summons you to his throne room.

[The Tin Man disappears behind the partition. The others freeze.]

Tin Man: If you please, great and noble Sir, I am a Woodman, and I am made of tin. Therefore I have no heart and I cannot love. I pray you to give me a heart that I may be as other people are.

Wizard: Why should I do this?

Tin Man: If you please, sir, you should do this because I ask it of you, and because no one else can help me.

Wizard: I do not act simply because someone asks me to act. If you wish me to do as you ask, you must fulfill the condition I set before you. I demand that you kill the Wicked Witch of the West.

Scarecrow: Kill the Wicked Witch of the West? But, sir, I cannot do that! I have no idea how such a thing could be done!

[After a moment or two of silence, the Tin Man returns sadly to his comrades.]

Tin Man: Alas! Alas! Oh, my friends, I am doomed to live the rest of my life—which you will agree must be a very long time indeed, as I am made of tin!—without being able to love! Oh, alas, alas!

Lion: That Wizard is not a good wizard, he is a cruel wizard! If he summons me, I shall answer him with my fiercest roar! I shall slash him with the full length of my terrible claws! I shall pounce upon him with the full force of my fearsome strength!

[The gong sounds.]

Soldier: Come, Lion, the Wizard summons you into his presence.

Lion *[moaning loudly]*: NOOOOOOO! Oh, help! I shall never return, I know it! SAAAAVE ME! Please! *[And thus weeping and gnashing his teeth and holding onto his tail for dear life, the Lion disappears behind the partition.]*

Please, your great and w-w-w-wonderful w-w-w-wizardness, I am a lowly lion—a cowardly lowly lion. I am afraid of

EVERYTHING. And I have come to beg you to give me courage, so that I might become in reality what men call me: The King of Beasts.

Wizard: Why should I give you courage?

Lion: You should give me courage because, of all Wizards you are the greatest, and you alone have the p-p-p-power to grant my request.

Wizard: Very well. I shall grant your request. Bring me proof that the Wicked Witch of the West is dead, and you shall have all the courage you shall ever need.

Lion: You demand I bring you proof that the Wicked Witch is dead? But-but-but...

[After a few moments, the Lion returns to his friends.]

Lion *[angry and disgusted]*: It is no use. He demands that I bring him proof that the Wicked Witch of the West is dead before he will help me.

Dorothy *[sadly]*: What shall we do now?

Lion: There is only one thing we can do, and that is to go to the land of the West and seek out the Wicked Witch.

Dorothy: But suppose we cannot?

Lion: Then I shall never have courage.

Scarecrow: And I shall never have brains.

Tin Man: And I shall never have a heart.

Dorothy *[starting to cry]*: And I shall never see Aunt Emily and Uncle Henry again!

[Her friends gather around to comfort her. After a few moments she recovers and says, sighing & half-sobbing:]

Dorothy: I suppose we must try it. But I am sure I do not want to kill anybody, even to see Aunt Emily again.

Lion: I will go with you, but I'm too much of a coward to kill the Witch.

Scarecrow: I will go with you also. But I shall not be of much help to you, as I am such a fool.

Tin Man: I haven't the heart to harm even a Witch. But if you go, I certainly shall go with you.

ACT III, Scene 1

[A very despondent group of friends approaches the Guardian of the Gate from SR. He unlocks their spectacles, placing each pair carefully in the big box. Then he politely "opens" the gate. All four sigh deeply in unison.]

Dorothy: Which road leads to the Wicked Witch of the West?

Guardian: There is no road. No one ever wishes to go that way.

Dorothy: Then how are we to find her?

Guardian: Oh, that will be no problem. Just go West into the Country of the Winkies, and when she learns that you are there, she will take you all and make you her slaves.

Scarecrow: Well, perhaps—and perhaps not. For you must know that we mean to destroy her utterly.

Guardian: Oh! That is different! No one has ever destroyed her before, so I naturally thought she would make slaves of you as she has of the rest. But you must take care, for she is wicked and fierce, and she may not allow you to destroy her. Keep going West, where the sun sets, and you cannot fail to find her.

Four Friends *[all together, talking over one another]*: Oh, thank you, Sir. We shall be very careful indeed.

[They walk across to SL and out the door. We see a tall, black, pointed hat gradually appearing above the partition. It is the Wicked Witch of the West,

standing on a stepladder so that she appears to be standing in one of her towers. The Witch has only one eye; the other is covered with a black patch cut in the shape of a black cat (if we can manage it)].

Witch: Who is this I spy walking into my land of the West?!!? A lion. A straw man. A tin man. A little girl of flesh and blood. And not one of them did I allow permission to enter my country! *[She takes out a silver whistle and blows once upon it.]*

[Teacher to audience: And now, you must all howl and yelp and growl like a great pack of wolves! (After a minute of this, the Teacher calms everyone down.) Meanwhile, the Witch has been looking down into her "courtyard," as if she is being surrounded by her wolf pack.]

Witch: Now, my pretty wolves. Go to those people coming into my lands, and tear them to pieces! I will not make them my slaves, for one is of tin, and one is of straw, and one is a beast, and one is a girl, and none of them is fit to work. Now go! Go!

The Four Friends open the door on floor level at SL and walk out into the center. They pause as if listening.

Scarecrow: Listen! It sounds like a huge pack of ravening wolves is headed our way! What shall we do?

Tin Man *[swinging his ax, as if limbering up to chop wood]*: This is my fight, so stay here and I will go to meet them before they arrive. It will be a little surprise for them, I imagine. *[very puffed up and macho]*

[He strides manfully to the door at SR and "slams" it open. We hear lots of yowls and crashes, made in fact by the Tin Man, from behind the door. Then silence. The Tin Man then re-enters through the same door.]

Tin Man: It was a good fight, my friends.

[They continue on down the aisle, SL. The Witch once again mounts her "tower," spying all around.]

Witch: Aargh!!! My beautiful wolves all dead! How dare they! I'll fix them! *[She takes out the silver whistle and blows twice upon it. The Teacher asks the audience to caw and cackle like huge crows. After a minute of this, she settles them down.]*

Witch *[gazing down and around her "tower"]*: Ah, my lovely crows! You are indeed the ugliest flying creatures I have ever seen! Fly at once to those strangers and tear them to pieces!

[The Four Friends are approaching the stage from the center aisle. They all stop mid-way and peer into the distant sky.]

Dorothy: Oh, my goodness! Look! It is a huge flock of crows of tremendous size and evil aspect! They must have been sent by the Witch!

Scarecrow: Never fear, Miss Dorothy. This is my battle. *[He marches up the center aisle and through the door at SL. There is a cacophony of screeches and bangings, made in fact by the Scarecrow. Then the Scarecrow returns, dusting off his hands and looking extremely pleased with himself.]*

Scarecrow: Have no fears or worries, Miss Dorothy. Those wicked crows will bother us no longer. Indeed, they will no longer bother anyone.

Dorothy: That is a relief to us all, my friend. But I must confess that I find myself fatigued from these attacks. Might we sit here and rest awhile? I have bread and cheese in my basket.

Tin Man: Why, of course, Miss Dorothy. But if you don't mind, I think I will stand and rest. It is much more comfortable for metal people if we don't have to bend and sit.

[They arrange themselves mid-way to the stage in the center aisle. Meanwhile, the Witch once more appears in her tower. She peers around the auditorium, bringing her gaze at last to the area beneath and around the tower. She gasps.]

Witch: My crows! My lovely, evil crows! I'll fix them this time! If they think their troubles are over, I'll make them think twice! *[She blows on the whistle three times.]*

[The Teacher instructs the audience to make loud buzzing sounds like angry bees. After a moment of this, she calms them down.]

Tin Man: Listen! I hear a sound as of angry bees. Lots of angry bees.

Scarecrow: I fear you are correct, my friend. And, though I know I have no brains and therefore am not so good at thinking, I am beginning to wonder where all these creatures are coming from. Do you think the Witch has seen us, and is sending them all to attack us?

Lion: Never mind that now! We must get to safety before we are stung to death.

Scarecrow: Look, my friends, look! It is a haystack! Quickly now—Miss Dorothy and Lion, burrow into the hay and that will protect you from the bees. Tin Man and I need have no fears from them.

[Dorothy and the Lion scoot into one of the aisles, underneath the legs of the children sitting there. The Scarecrow lies down on the floor at the start of the aisle, to protect them. The Tin Man stands tall, while the audience makes buzzing noises, gradually getting softer and softer until finally there is silence.]

Tin Man: You may come out now, my friends! All the evil bees are dead. They tried to sting me, but their stingers fell out when they came into contact with my metal. And you know, once a bee—even an evil bee—loses its stinger, it dies. Alas.

Lion: Alas, indeed! Those bees deserved to die, frightening Miss Dorothy like that!

Dorothy: And Toto, too!

Lion: Yes, and Toto, too! What an awful thing to do to anyone!

Dorothy: If you don't mind, I think I would like to stay here for just a little longer. Just until my heart stops pounding so hard and fast!

Tin Man: Ah. If only I had a heart to pound. You creatures with hearts simply do not realize how fortunate you are.

[Once again, the Witch appears in her "tower." She again peers all around the auditorium and finally sees the "piles of dead bees."]

Witch *[having a real fit!]*: That's it! That's really it! The complete and utter end! *[calling loudly]* Slaves! I demand that my slaves appear! Slaves!

[The Witch looks down into her courtyard as if it is filled with Winkies.]

Witch: You there! You Winkies! My slaves! I command you to find those intruders and kill them all! Now go!

[The Teacher encourages the audience to make marching noises with their feet.]

Dorothy: Oh, my! Oh, my! What are we to do?

Lion: Why, there's only one thing to do! *[He gives a mighty roar at the "Winkies."]* There! That will take care of the Winkies! No one wants to take a chance with a lion, even though he be the world's greatest coward!

[The Witch, who has been watching all this from her tower, now screams in frustration. She comes down from her tower and out from behind the partition.]

Witch: You think you have won! Well, I have one more trick up my sleeve, and that you will not escape!

[She looks down in her sleeve and takes out a cap covered in jewels.]

Witch: When I wear this cap and say the magic charm, it will cause to happen whatever I command!

[She puts on the cap and stands on her left foot, reciting slowly.]

Witch: Ep-pe, pep-pe, kak-ke!

[She switches to her right foot.]

Witch: Hil-lo, hol-lo, hel-lo!

[She now stands on both feet.]

Witch: Ziz-zy, zuz-zy, zik!

[There is a low rumbling from off-stage, and the lights flicker on and off.]

Witch *[in a very spooky voice]*: Cap of Magic, I command you to bash the Tin Man upon the rocks!

[The Tin Man moans and twirls toward the door, SR, and falls in a heap.]

Witch: Cap of Magic, I command you to toss that Scarecrow into the trees!

[The Scarecrow twirls and whirls about, moaning and crying out, and lands on a couple of empty chairs near the Tin Man.]

Witch: Cap of Magic, I command you to bring to me the Lion and the girl, Dorothy!

[The Lion and Dorothy move toward the steps at SR as if pulled by an irresistible and very strong force. They call for help and cry out, all the way, until they fall in a heap at the feet of the Witch.]

Witch: Lion, I command you to go into that cage *[pointing to the door at SL]* and lock yourself inside! Girl, I command you to.... *[seeing the mark of the kiss on her forehead]*... *[Aside]* But what is this? It is the mark of the Witch of the North!...Go into my kitchen, girl, and start peeling potatoes! There are plenty of dishes to wash! And scrub the floor! Now go! *[wicked laughter. As Dorothy turns to walk off behind the partition, the Witch obviously spies the silver slippers. She gasps! Once Dorothy is behind the partition, she says to herself:]*

Witch: The Silver Shoes! They belonged to my sister, the Wicked Witch of the East! This creature does not deserve them! She does not even know their power! I must get them from her. I must have them! Then my power will be increased one hundred fold! No one will be able to stand in my way! I must have them! I must!

[At an inconspicuous time, the Tin Man and the Scarecrow sneak through the door, SR.]

ACT III, Scene 2

[Dorothy is at SR, wearing an apron and on her hands & knees with a bucket, scrubbing the floor. The Witch comes out from behind the partition and walks in a witchly way to the door at SL, which she cracks open. Dorothy watches her but does not stop scrubbing.]

Witch: Now, you obstreperous creature! Are you ready to pull my little cart like a horse?

Lion *[from behind the door]*: ROAR!

Witch: I warn you! If you do not cooperate and pull my little cart like a horse, you will never come out of this cage!

Lion: ROAR! I will never allow myself to be harnessed like a horse! And if you come in here, I will bite you! ROAR!

Witch: Very well then! If you will not allow yourself to be harnessed like a horse, I shall starve you! You shall have nothing to eat until you do as I wish!

[The Witch stomps off, back behind the partition. Dorothy scrubs for a moment longer, then looks around. She quietly stands and tip-toes over to the door at SL.]

Dorothy: Lion! It is I, Dorothy!

Lion: Ah, my friend! How are you being treated, Miss Dorothy?

Dorothy: In truth, she does not treat me too badly, though she does try again and again to make me give her my silver slippers. Otherwise, I work hard, but although she is not kind and she yells quite a bit, she does not touch me. Here—I have brought you something to eat. *[She takes a crust of bread out of her apron pocket.]*

Lion: Oh, my dear friend. The only thing that keeps me from starving is the bread you bring me. I don't know how you can be in her presence every day, all day long, and how you can sleep soundly at night knowing that she is under the very same roof. I am sure that I could never be so calm as

	you are, Miss Dorothy, for as you know, I have no courage whatsoever. SIGH!
Dorothy:	She shall return in a moment—I must go back to the kitchen. But first I'll pick a few of these lovely wild flowers here. I am certain that she does not know of their existence, for she cannot abide flowers at all and kills them with a magic spell whenever she sees them. So if she asks, I will not tell her where these came from.

[While Dorothy is occupied picking the flowers, the Witch creeps out from behind the partition, pantomiming carrying a brick.]

Witch *[softly]*:	Now we shall see who shall have those slippers! I shall put this invisible brick right here, where she will certainly trip over it when she comes back to the kitchen. And when she does trip, I shall pull off the shoes!

[The Witch crouches against the partition, seemingly out of sight of Dorothy, who slowly walks back toward the "kitchen" holding her flowers and humming a little tune. As she comes to the invisible brick, she trips. The Witch jumps up and grabs one of the shoes off her foot.]

Dorothy *[incensed]*: Give me back my shoe!

Witch *[gleefully]*: I will not! For it is now my shoe, and not yours!

Dorothy:	You are a wicked creature! You have no right to take my shoe from me!
Witch:	I shall keep it, just the same! And *[laughing, cackling]* moreover, some day I shall get the other one from you, too!

[This makes Dorothy so angry that she picks up the bucket of water and dashes it over the Witch. The Witch cries out in great fear and begins to shrink away.]

Witch *[screaming]*: Now see what you have done! I am melting, melting, melting away!

Dorothy: Oh, indeed, I am very sorry! I never meant to hurt you!

Witch *[wailing in despair]*: Did you not know that water would mean the end of me?

Dorothy: No, I did not, for how could I?

Witch *[fading away]*: In a few moments I shall be all melted away, and you shall have my castle all to yourself. I have been wicked in my day, but I never thought a little girl like you would ever be able to melt me and end my beautiful wicked deeds. Oh, look out!! Here I go!!

[The Witch slinks away behind the partition. Dorothy looks at the floor as if looking at a mess and throws another bucket of water over it. She picks up her silver shoe, wipes it off, and puts it back on. She then runs back to the Lion's cage, opens the door with a key, and the Lion bounds out.]

Lion: AAHHRR! *[big roaring stretch]* It feels so good to be out of that cage! *[looking around]* But, Miss Dorothy, how do I come to be free? Where is the Witch? What has happened?

Dorothy *[distressed]*: Oh, Lion, you will never guess! I was walking back to the kitchen with my flowers, and the Witch tricked me, and I fell down, and I dropped my flowers, and she grabbed one of my slippers when I fell, and then I got really mad, and I threw the bucket of water at her, and then she yelled at me, and then she started to melt! She melted! Oh, Lion, it was awful! She melted into an ugly brown puddle, and it smelled just like rotten eggs!

Lion: Oh, my! This is indeed… well, it is remarkable. Who would ever have thought that a witch would melt! My, my. But you are well, and I am well, and now the Winkies will also be well, for they will no longer be slaves!

Dorothy: Yes, yes, that is true! And now we can leave and return to the Wizard!

Lion: Oh, what a shame our fine comrades cannot join us. What do you think happened to them?

Dorothy: You are right, Lion! We must endeavor to discover what happened to our friends, and we must save them if at all possible. I'll ask the Winkies to search for them. I'm certain they'll help us, once they've learned that the Witch is dead and that they're no longer slaves!

Lion: Good! Good! And now, Miss Dorothy, if you don't mind, bread and cheese may be fine food for people, but for a lion they are but poor substitutes for a real meal. And I am HUNGRY! Let us search the Witch's kitchen and see what we can find. We deserve a banquet!

[They embrace and skip off through the door, SR, chanting, "A banquet, a banquet, we shall have a banquet!"]

ACT III, Scene 3

[Dorothy, the Lion, the Scarecrow, and the Tin Man enter joyfully from the SR door. They walk across to the aisle, SL, and walk down it as they are talking.]

Tin Man: Oh, I was in terrible shape when the Winkies found me—terrible shape! In fact, technically I was in no shape at all, as I was in pieces! Pieces, mind you, for the Winged Monkeys had thrown me over a high cliff onto the rocks below, and the crash broke me into bits! And then it rained and I rusted, and of course I had lost my oil can in the crash! But then the kindly Winkies found me, and picked up all my pieces, and took me to a tinsmith, and look at me now! I do believe that I must shine so bright in the sun that it would hurt one's eyes to look at me!

Scarecrow: I'm sure that must be the case, my friend, for you are truly something to behold! But at least your pieces were actual pieces! The Winged Monkeys ripped out all my straw and tossed it through the forest. And then they threw my shirt over one tree, and my trousers over another, and my hat into a pond, and my poor head into a thorn bush! But the Winkies found all my garments and stitched me back together and stuffed me with fresh, clean straw. And here I am, good as new!

Tin Man: It certainly seems so! No doubt, if I had a heart I would be truly able to appreciate your beauty!

Scarecrow: And if I had a brain, I could have figured out a way for us to have avoided the Winged Monkeys altogether.

Lion: And if I had courage, I would have been able to save Miss Dorothy from the rough work the Witch put her to.

Dorothy: But now, we need to get back to Oz—so that you can have your heart, and you can have your brain, and you can have your courage, and I can get back to Kansas. *[We hear a little bark from Toto (actually from Dorothy).]* Oh, yes, Toto, and you, too!

[By this point, they are starting to walk down the center aisle.]

Scarecrow: Of course you are quite correct, Miss Dorothy. We are following the path set out for us by the Winkies, and I do believe we should be in the vicinity of the City of Emeralds before very long.

Lion: Oh, look! There it is! Right in front of us!

[They run and skip down the center aisle, up the steps SL, and knock on the partition. Their knock is answered by the Guard.]

Guard: Who goes there?

Dorothy: It is I, Dorothy, the small and meek, and my three companions.

Guard: But the Great and Terrible Oz instructed you to go to the Land of the Winkies and to kill the Wicked Witch of the West!

Dorothy: That is what we have done! Look! *[She pulls the Witch's hat from her basket.]* Here is the Witch's hat! We have melted the Witch and freed all the Winkies, and now the Land of the West is a happy land!

Guard: Why... why so you have! So it would appear! Well, then I suppose I must apprise the Great and Mighty Oz of your arrival.

[The Guard once again fastens spectacles on each of them.]

Guard: Now. Wait here until I return for you.

[They wait patiently, looking at one another, and looking all around, adjusting their spectacles and pointing out the sights to one another.]

Guard: You are to follow me, if you please.

[He leads them through the door SR, pulling the end partition over to cover the entry way. When they are all off the stage, two actors bring the great Throne of Oz onto the stage and place it in the center of the stage. Behind the Throne, they place a tall stand covered with a green curtain, so that the Throne is centered in front of it. It must now be possible for someone to walk from the door, SR, to the space behind the curtain, without being seen by the audience. Once the throne has been placed, the social hall door, SR, opens and the Four Companions slowly enter the social hall. Behind them, but out of sight, we hear the voice of the Guard.]

Guard: That's right... just walk on into the Throne Room. Oz the Great and Terrible is waiting to speak with you... Well, go on now! Don't hesitate!

[They timidly approach the area in front of the Throne.]

Scarecrow: Well, now, this is an interesting situation. The Throne appears to be empty! I wonder where the Wizard might be?

[From off-stage comes a loud, stentorian voice.]

Wizard: I am Oz, the Great and Terrible. Who are these lowly creatures that pester me so?

Dorothy: If you please, your Oz-ship, it is I, Dorothy, the meek and powerless. I have returned from the Land of the West, having killed the Wicked Witch as you commanded. Where are you?

Wizard: I am everywhere. But to the eyes of common mortals I am invisible. Why do you interrupt my important business?

Dorothy: If you please, we have come to claim your promise, O Oz.

Wizard: What promise?

Dorothy: You promised to send me back to Kansas when the Wicked Witch was destroyed.

Scarecrow:	And you promised to give me brains.
Tin Man:	And you promised to give me a heart.
Lion:	And you promised to give me courage.
Wizard:	And I commanded you to bring me proof that the Wicked Witch of the West is actually dead.
Dorothy:	Oh, yes, she is most definitely dead, for I melted her with a bucket of water. And look, here is her hat, which I have brought back for you, your Oz-ship.
Wizard:	Dear me. How very sudden. Well, you must return tomorrow, for I must have time to think all this over.
Tin Man:	You've had plenty of time already!
Scarecrow:	We shan't wait a day longer.
Lion:	You must keep your promises to Dorothy and to the rest of us! ROAR! ROAR! ROAR!

[At the Lion's roars, the green curtain behind the Throne begins to quiver and shake, and finally falls over, revealing the Guard with a microphone.]

Lion *[bounding toward the Guard]*: Who are you?

Guard *[into the microphone]*: I am Oz, the Great and Terrible, but don't strike me—please don't—and I'll do anything you want me to!!

[The Four gaze at him in surprise and dismay.]

Dorothy:	But I thought Oz was a great Wizard.
Tin Man:	And I thought he was a powerful Wizard.
Lion:	And I thought he was a terrible Wizard.
Scarecrow:	And I thought he was an all-wise Wizard.
Wizard:	No, I'm afraid you are all wrong. I have been making believe.
Dorothy:	Making believe! Are you not a great Wizard?
Wizard:	Hush, my dear. Don't speak so loud, or you will be overheard, and I should be ruined. I'm supposed to be a great Wizard.

Dorothy:	And aren't you?
Wizard:	Not a bit of it, my dear. I'm just a common man.
Scarecrow:	You're more than that. *[very sad and angry]* You're a-a-a humbug!
Wizard:	Exactly so! I am a humbug.
Tin Man:	But this is terrible! If you're a humbug, how shall I ever get my heart?
Lion:	Or I my courage?
Scarecrow:	Or I my brains?
Wizard:	My dear friends, I pray you not to speak of these little things. Think of me! Think of the terrible trouble I am in at being found out!
Dorothy:	Doesn't anyone else know you're a humbug?
Wizard:	No one knows it but you four—and I, myself, of course. I have fooled everyone for so long that I thought I should never be found out. It was truly a great mistake on my part to ever allow you into the Throne Room. Usually I will not see even my subjects, and so they believe I am something terrible.
Scarecrow:	Really, you ought to be ashamed of yourself for being such a humbug.
Wizard:	I am. I certainly am. But it was the only thing I could do. You see, I was born in Omaha…
Dorothy:	Why, that isn't very far from Kansas!
Wizard:	No, but it's very far from here. *[He shakes his head sadly.]* When I grew up I decided to join a circus and travel the country. But I had to think of something to do so a circus would want to take me on, so finally I decided to become a balloonist.
Dorothy:	What is a balloonist?

Wizard:	That is a person who goes up in a balloon on circus day, so as to draw a crowd of people together and get them to pay to see the circus.
Dorothy:	Oh, I've heard of that.
Wizard:	So I studied hard. For, you know, in order to be a balloonist, one must learn all about weather phenomena, and how warm air acts differently from cold air, and about special gases, and about wind currents, and all such things. I found an experienced balloonist who took me on as an apprentice for a while. But I worked so hard that soon I was ready to set off on my own. So I did, and a traveling circus hired me on, and for many years I was very happy. It is nice to look at the world from up in the basket of a balloon.
	Well, one day I went up in a balloon and the ropes got twisted, so that I couldn't come down again. The balloon went way up above the clouds, so far that a current of air struck it and carried it many, many miles. I traveled for a day and a night, and when I awoke on the second day, I found myself floating over a strange and beautiful country.
	The balloon came down gradually so that I was not hurt a bit. But I found myself in the midst of a strange people who, seeing me descend from the clouds, thought I was a great Wizard. Of course I let them think so, because they were afraid of me and promised to do anything I wished them to. So I ordered them to build this beautiful city, and this they did willingly and well. The land was so green that I called it the City of Emeralds. And I made it the law that everyone who entered the gate had to wear special spectacles that would make everything in the city appear to be green.
Dorothy:	But isn't everything here green?
Wizard:	No more than in any other place. But when you look at the world through green spectacles, of course everything you see looks green to you.
	Now, one of my greatest fears was the Witches, for while I had no magical powers at all, I soon found out that the

Witches were really able to do wonderful things. There were four of them in this country, and they ruled the people in the North and South and East and West. The Witches of the North and South are good witches, but the Witches of the East and West were terribly wicked. Had they not thought I was more powerful than they themselves, they would surely have destroyed me.

As it is, I have lived in deadly fear of them for many years. So you can imagine how pleased I was when I heard your house had fallen on the Wicked Witch of the East. And I am delighted that you have melted the Wicked Witch of the West. But I am ashamed to say that I cannot keep my promises. *[He shakes his head sadly.]*

Dorothy:	I think you are a very bad man.
Wizard:	Oh, no, my dear. I'm really a very good man. But, alas, I am a very bad Wizard, I must admit.
Scarecrow:	Can't you give me brains?
Wizard:	Oh, you don't need brains. You are learning something every day.
Scarecrow:	That may be true, but I shall nevertheless be very unhappy unless you give me brains.
Tin Man:	And I shall be very unhappy unless you give me a heart.
Wizard:	Oh, now, I think you are wrong to want a heart. Having hearts makes most people most unhappy.
Tin Man:	That must be a matter of opinion. For my part, I will bear all the unhappiness without a murmur of complaint, if you will only give me the heart.
Lion:	And what about my courage?
Wizard:	You have plenty of courage, I am sure! What you lack is confidence in yourself. There is no living thing that is not afraid when it faces danger. True courage is in facing danger when you are afraid, and that is the kind of courage that you have in plenty.

Lion: Perhaps I have, but I'm scared just the same. I shall really be very unhappy unless you give me the sort of courage that makes one forget he is afraid.

Wizard: Oh, very well! If you are all three prepared for a little minor unpleasantness, I will endeavor to give you a brain, and you a heart, and you some courage. Scarecrow, step this way, please.

[The Wizard leads the Scarecrow behind the partition. We hear rattling, shuffling noises from behind the partition. When the Scarecrow reenters, the Wizard following closely behind, it is obvious that his head is bigger, stuffed with more straw.]

Dorothy *[curiously]*: What did you stuff his head with?

Wizard: Why, I stuffed his head with bran cereal, of course. Now he has bran-new brains.

Dorothy: How do you feel?

Scarecrow: I feel wise indeed! When I get used to my brains, I shall know everything!

Tin Man: What are those needles and pins sticking out of your head?

Lion: Why, that is proof of how sharp he is.

Tin Man: Wizard, you have done such a fine job on my friend that now I must ask you to proceed in giving me a heart.

Wizard: Very well. But I shall have to cut a little hole so that I might install it.

Tin Man: Oh, that won't hurt a bit! I don't feel anything at all, you know.

Wizard: Come along, then. *[He leads the Tin Man behind the partition. The sound of a drill (pretending to be a saw) is heard. The Tin Man leads the Wizard back into the Throne Room.]*

Tin Man: But is it a kind heart that you have given me?

Wizard: Oh, very!

Lion: And now for my courage!

Wizard [*reaching behind the Throne for a green bottle*]: Very well. Here. Drink.

Lion: What is it?

Wizard: Well, if it were inside you, it would be courage. You know, of course, that courage is always inside one. So this really cannot be called courage until you have swallowed it. Therefore, I advise you to drink it as soon as possible.

[The Lion drinks until the bottle is empty.]

Wizard: How do you feel now?

Lion: Full of courage!

Dorothy: And now is it my turn? I'm afraid no drink from a green bottle will get me back to Kansas.

Wizard: No, my dear, you are correct. But I do have an idea for getting you out of this country.

Dorothy: And back to Kansas?

Wizard: Well, I'm not sure about Kansas, for I haven't the faintest notion which way it lies. But the first thing is to cross the desert that surrounds this land, and then I think it should be easy to find your way home.

Dorothy: But how can I cross the desert?

Wizard: I'll tell you what I think. You see, when I came to this country it was in a balloon. You also came through the air, being carried by a cyclone. So I believe the best way to get across the desert will be through the air. Now, it is quite beyond my powers to create a cyclone, but I believe I can make a balloon. In fact, I still have the balloon that brought me here. And I do believe both of us will fit in the basket, and that the balloon itself is big enough to carry both of us.

[Toto barks.]

Dorothy:	Oh, yes, Toto, and you, too. I would not leave you. But sir, how can we travel in the balloon without the proper type of gas?
Wizard:	Remember what I told you, my dear. Gas is not the only way, though it is the best. However, hot air will also work to lift the balloon.
Dorothy:	And you said "we." What do you mean?
Wizard:	My child, I find that I am tired of being a humbug, and I am tired of staying shut up in these rooms day after day and year after year. So I think it is time for me to leave, as well. Our friend the Scarecrow is now so intelligent that I believe he will make a fine ruler for the Munchkins. So I plan to leave him in charge. Say good-bye to your friends, and we shall be on our way.
Dorothy:	Oh, my goodness! Good-bye, my friends, good-bye!

[The Wizard pushes the Throne aside to reveal a ladder draped in a large cloth. The ladder is not seen. At the foot of the ladder is a brightly painted basket, and attached to the basket is a helium balloon. The Wizard steps into the basket and takes hold of the balloon.]

Wizard:	Come, child, come! We have no time to waste! The balloon is beginning to rise!
Dorothy:	Wait! Wait! Toto has jumped out of my arms! *[She gets down on her hands and knees and searches beneath the Throne. Meanwhile the Wizard is lifting the basket slowly so that it appears he is rising into the air.]*
Wizard:	Dorothy! I cannot stop this machine!

Dorothy *[having found Toto and clutching him closely]*: Oh, alas! Help! Help!

[The others run around frantically, but the Wizard has stepped back between the sheets and disappeared.]

Dorothy *[sobbing]*: Oh, he is gone! And he was my only chance of getting back to Kansas! Now I shall never see Aunt Emily and Uncle Henry again!

[Slowly, behind the partition, at the same spot and on the same step-ladder used by the Wicked Witch of the West, Glinda the Good Witch of the South arises. The Scarecrow, Tin Man, and Lion all gasp.]

Scarecrow, Tin Man, and Lion: Dorothy! Look!

Dorothy *[following their pointing fingers]*: What... who are you?

Glinda: My name is Glinda, and I am the Good Witch of the South. I have heard from the good people of the north, and the east, and the west, that there is a new and powerful witch in our land, and that her name is Dorothy. But here I see Dorothy, and you appear to me to be only a young and very troubled girl. What can I do for you, my child?

Dorothy: Oh, begging your pardon, ma'am, but I don't suppose there is anything at all you can do for me. I never meant to come here, and I never meant to kill the Wicked Witch of the East or the Wicked Witch of the West, and all I ever wanted was to get back to Kansas, and now the Wizard has gone and I'll never get home, never, never, never. *[starting to sob again]*

Glinda: Bless your dear heart, child! I am sure I can tell you of a way to get back to Kansas. But first I must ensure that your friends are all taken care of. Scarecrow, what will you do when Dorothy has left us?

Scarecrow: I shall return to the Emerald City, for Oz has made me its ruler, and the people there like me. And now that I have brains, I am certain that I will make a most excellent ruler.

Glinda: Tin Man, what shall become of you when Dorothy leaves this country?

Tin Man: The Winkies in the Land of the West were very kind to me, and they wanted me to rule over them after the Wicked Witch was dead. I shall return to the Land of the Winkies, and we shall all deal very happily together I am sure, especially as I now have such a kind heart.

Glinda: And now, my courageous Lion, when Dorothy has returned to her own home, what shall become of you?

Lion:	Over the way there lies a grand old forest, and all the beasts that live there have asked me to become their King now that the Kalidahs are vanquished. So I shall return to the forest and take up my rightful role as King of the Beasts.
Dorothy:	It is good of you to take such a kind interest in my friends. But you have not yet explained to me how I am to get back to Kansas.
Glinda:	Why, bless your heart, child, your Silver Shoes will carry you back to Kansas. Had you known their power, you could have gone back to your Aunt Emily and Uncle Henry the very first day you came to this country.
Scarecrow:	But then I should not have had my wonderful brains! And I might have passed my whole life in the farmer's cornfield!
Tin Man:	And I should not have had my lovely heart. I might have stood and rusted in the forest until the end of the world.
Lion:	And I should have lived a coward forever. And no beast in all the forest would have had a good word to say to me.
Dorothy:	This is all true, and I am glad I was of use to these good friends. But now that each of them has been given what he has most desired, and each in addition is happy in having a kingdom to rule, I think I should like to go back to Kansas.
Glinda:	The Silver Shoes have wonderful powers. One of the most curious things about them is that they can carry you to any place in the world in three steps, and each step will be made in the wink of an eye. All you have to do is to knock the heels together three times and command the shoes to carry you wherever you wish to go.
Dorothy:	If that is so, I shall ask them to carry me back to Kansas at once. *[Dorothy throws her arms around the Lion's neck and pats his head and kisses him. She hugs and kisses the Tin Man, who is crying, and she oils his face once more. She hugs the Scarecrow tightly while she sobs. Glinda blows her a kiss. Dorothy holds Toto tightly in her arms, says one more goodbye, taps the heels of her shoes together three times, and says:]*

Dorothy: Take me home to Kansas!

[She twirls and twirls and jumps off the stage. Immediately all the players line up behind her, and all bow together.]

The End

www.ingramcontent.com/pod-product-compliance
Lightning Source LLC
Chambersburg PA
CBHW080454170426
43196CB00016B/2794